TWAYNE'S WORLD AUTHORS SERIES

A Survey of the World's Literature

Sylvia E. Bowman, Indiana University

GENERAL EDITOR

SPAIN

Gerald Wade, Vanderbilt University

EDITOR

Baltasar Gracián

TWAS 337

Drawing by Carderera in the Biblioteca Nacional, Madrid

Baltasar Gracián

Baltasar Gracián

By VIRGINIA RAMOS FOSTER
Phoenix College

TWAYNE PUBLISHERS
A DIVISION OF G. K. HALL & CO., BOSTON

Library of Congress Cataloging in Publication Data

Foster, Virginia Ramos.
  Baltasar Gracián.

  (Twayne's world authors series, TWAS 337. Spain)
  Bibliography: p. 159-66.
  1.   Gracián y Morales, Baltasar, 1601-1658.
PQ6398.G4F6   868'.3'09   74-19235
ISBN 0-8057-23986

MANUFACTURED IN THE UNITED STATES OF AMERICA

A vos, querido David: máximo compañero, buen entendedor, eminente crítico, hombre juicioso y notante.

Contents

About the Author

Virginia Ramos Foster is Professor of Spanish at Phoenix College. She obtained a Ph.D. in Spanish from the University of Missouri in 1966, where she served as an instructor of Spanish. Her specialized preparation has been in the area of seventeenth-century literature, with an emphasis on literary theory. Dr. Foster has traveled extensively in Latin America and has spent several periods in Buenos Aires, where she has conducted research on the Argentine theater, for which she has had fellowship support from the Organization of American States. In addition to her publications on the Argentine theater and regular reviews for *Books Abroad*, Dr. Foster has collaborated with David William Foster on *Manual of Hispanic Bibliography*, *Research Guide to Argentine Literature*, and *Modern Latin American Literature*. She is also coauthor with him of the TWAS study on *Luis de Góngora*.

Preface

The aim of this monograph on the works of Baltasar Gracián is to attempt to give a panoramic characterization of Gracián's works as representative of seventeenth-century Spanish literature of the Baroque period. The ultimate goal is not only to study the artistic uniqueness of the Jesuit and his writings but also to trace the development of his humanistic ideas which convey his vision of mankind and the world. Besides trying to convey an understanding of the general features of Gracián's works, the study offers an interpretation of the underlying organization of the literary theory of *The Mind's Wit and Art*. Gracián's literary criticism is randomly presented in his writings, at least from the point of view of contemporary criticism; the intent here has been to summarize the major precepts for the modern reader. In the case of the allegorical novel *The Master Critic*, an attempt has been made to go beyond pseudophilosophic content by a discussion of the underlying literary structure and the distinct unity or patterning of the work.

In addition to the two chapters apiece devoted to Gracián's two major works, a final chapter focuses on Gracián's other writings, which have as their unifying theme his overriding concern with the quality of man's life and the ways in which he must educate and conduct himself in order to be a complete human being.

Unless otherwise stated, all quotations from the works are taken from the edition by Arturo del Hoyo, *Obras completas*, fourth edition (Madrid: Aguilar, 1960). For reasons of space, in many instances texts are quoted only in translation.

Chronology

1601	Baptized January 8 at Belmonte near Calatayud. This is assumed to be his date of birth because of the ancient Spanish custom of baptizing the child on the date of his birth.
-ca. 1601 -ca. 1619	Spends his formative years in Toledo with his uncle Antonio Gracián, chaplain in the Chapel of San Pedro de los Reyes, where the young Gracián pursues his studies of humanities and philosophy. From 1616 to 1619 he studies with the Jesuits at their school in Zaragoza.
1619	Enters the novitiate of the Jesuits in Tarragona on May 30 at the age of eighteen. At this time, his "purity of blood" (i.e., pure Spanish lineage free of Jewish or Moorish ancestry) is proved.
1620	Writes the necrology for Brother Bartolomé Vallsebre of the Order; this represents the first known text by Gracián.
1621	First perpetual vows taken on May 21.
1621- 1623	Studies philosophy at the College of Catalatayud.
1623- 1627	Pursues theology studies in Zaragoza. Internal conflicts in the order on the provincial level.
1624	Writes the necrology for Father García de Alabiano; his second known text.
1626	Serves as secretary to the Vice-Rector, Blas de Vaylo.
1627- 1630	Professor of grammar at the Jesuit School in Calatayud; he also may have taught rhetoric.
1627	Ordained a priest.
1630- 1631	In Valencia March 30 to March 30 to complete this third probationary period preceding his public and apostolic life

as a Jesuit. Completes this period on March 5 with only a *sed parum satisfecit* due to the anti-Aragonese sentiment of his superiors, although Gracián had been an exemplary student.

1631-1633 Rapid rise to success in Lérida as Professor of theology and adviser to the rector.

1633-1636 Professor of languages and philosophy at the University of Gandía.

1635 Solemn profession of the four vows.

1636 Back in his beloved Aragón, in Huesca. Formation of the friendship with the famous humanist don Vincencio Juan de Lastanosa.

1637 First edition of *El héroe* (The Hero), published under the pseudonym of Lorenzon Gracián, *Infanzón* ("nobleman") without permission of the order and with a dedication to his friend Lastanosa.

1638 Reprimanded for his insolence and rebellion by the provincial general.

1639 Second edition of *El héroe* published with permission, but again under the pseudonym of Lorenzo Gracián.

1640 Confessor to Francesco María Carofa, Duke of Nochera and Viceroy of Aragón in Zaragoza. April and May in Madrid at the court, where he writes his first protest of court life.

Formation of friendship with the poet Antonio Hurtado de Mendoza, whom he later praises in the *Agudeza* (The Mind's Wit . . .). Publishes *El político* (The Politician), dedicated to Nochera, under the pseudonym of Lorenzo Gracián. This is the year of national upheavel with the revolt of Cataluña.

1641 Nochera arrested and imprisoned for his sympathetic support of Cataluña. Gracián in Madrid, where he preaches with great success.

1642 Death of Duke of Nochera and publication of *Arte de ingenio* (Art of Ingenuity) under the name of Lorenço Gracián. Became Vice-Rector of the society's House of Probation in Tarragona, a post held until 1644.

1644 Confessor and preacher at the novitiate in Valencia. Becomes object of hostility when he reads in a sermon a letter that he professed to have received from hell.

1646   Back in Huesca. Publishes *El discreto* (The Discreet Man) under the name of Lorenzo Gracián with permission, although the General of the order instructs him to stop writing and publishing more books. Becomes chaplain to the army of don Diego Felipe de Guzmán, Marqués of Leganés, who was fighting to save Lérida from the French. After the great slaughter on November 21, Gracián was acclaimed *Padre de la Victoria* ("Priest of Victory"). The formation of a friendship with the Portuguese nobleman and soldier Pablo de Parada.

1647   Publishes *El oráculo manual y arte de prudencia* (The Oracle, A Manual of the Art of Prudence), again under the pseudonym Lorenzo Gracián.

1648   The expanded and definitive edition of the *Arte de ingenio*, called the *Agudeza y arte de ingenio* (The Mind's Wit and Art) Gracián has become a famous literary critic and major spokesman of conceptism.

1649   In Huesca, as a professor of grammar, philosophy and moral theology.

1651   Professor of Sacred Scripture in Zaragoza. Publishes the first part of *El criticón* (The Master Critic) under the new pseudonym of García de Marlones (an anagram of his own name) and with the support of a new patron, Pablo de Parada; the book is censured.

1652   Start of a literary and personal feud with his friend, the Aragonese writer and Latinist, Manuel de Salinas (Lastanosa's cousin). English translation of *The Hero* by Sir J. Sheffington.

1653   Publication of the second part of the *Criticón* under pseudonym of Lorenzo Gracián.

1654   Publication of one of the most important anthologies of poetry of seventeenth-century Spain, *Poesías varias de grandes ingenios españoles* of Josef Alfay. It has been thought that Gracián wrote the prologue and made the selections.

1655   Publication of *El comulgatorio* (The Communion Book) under his own name.

1657   Publication of the third part of the *Criticón* in Madrid under the name of Lorenzo Gracián.

1658   Severe censure by the order for his rebelliousness and for the *Criticón;* sentenced to fast on bread and water as penance. Relieved of his professorship of Sacred Scripture at Zaragosa and exiled to Graus. Petitions to leave the order and join a monastic community. Dies on December 6.

CHAPTER 1

The Life and Times of Baltasar Gracián

I The Political Situation

THE period of Gracián's life (1601–1658) spanned most of the reign of two kings, Philip III (1598–1621) and Philip IV (1621–1665), with the greater part of his life falling in the period of the latter ruler, known as Philip the Great, the monarch who witnessed and supported the definitive maturation of arts and letters in the Golden Age of Spain. In contrast to such brilliance, the political life of the times was a disaster, with Spain falling into political impotence by the end of the seventeenth century. (Her decline, of course, was only a matter of time after the destruction of the Spanish Armada in 1588). During the reign of Philip III power was delegated to his favorite, the avaricious Duke of Lerma, whose regime suffered severe economic depression, the debasement of Spanish coinage, a crushing tax system, and the expulsion of the *moriscos*, the Moorish working class of Spain. The Duke of Lerma did however manage to effect cordial relations between Spain's enemies: England, France, and the Dutch. But entanglements continued in Ireland, Italy, and North Africa, the Turkish pirates caused trouble in the Mediterranean, and the defense of the Catholic cause during the Thirty Years' War (1630–1659) was disastrous. Corruption, poverty, hypocrisy, and a general disintegration of moral values marked the era, in spite of the fervent profession of religion. The rich church, a spendthrift, nonproductive court, legions of idle aristocrats, social parasites, beggars, prostitutes, and an ethic that minimized the value of work dominated the scene. It was during this time that Góngora was writing his difficult poetry, Lope de Vega his prodigious dramas, and Quevedo his incisive *Buscón* and the *Dreams*.

15

Philip IV was only sixteen when he inherited the throne, which he turned over at once to his favorite, the Count-Duke of Olivares; this irascible, dictatorial gentleman ruled for twenty-two years. He sought to maintain the traditional policy of Spanish imperialism in Europe and centralized absolutism in Spain. Matters of government worsened as constant wars and the extravagant court drained Spain's resources. Philip IV was known for his love of pleasure, his scandalous extramarital affairs, and his outright disdain of Christian morality. The country faced severe losses at the hands of the French, Dutch and English. In addition, the country suffered political and social unrest. The Catalonian revolt after 1640 was really a major revolution; peasants rose against the Spanish soldiers, capured Barcelona and murdered the Viceroy. The Catalans formed a republic and placed themselves under the protection of the French monarchy. It was not until 1659 that Philip IV regained control of the province through the Peace of the Pyrenees. The unity of Spain was further destroyed by the revolt in Lisbon and the subsequent independence of Portugal.

The disintegration of the Spanish empire was in full movement, as the country continued to lose lands and power to more aggressive nations. In essence, this was the painful course of history of the Spain in which Gracián and other writers and artists lived and suffered, many of them recording their anguish and concern in their works. This distressing situation was especially pertinent to Gracián in that the corrupt Court, his native Aragón (which Gracián saw as a spiritual antidote to the court), and the disastrous Catalalonian wars played a significant role in his life and his writings.[1]

II   Religious and Cultural Milieu[2]

Baltasar Gracián was a member of the Jesuits, the Society of Jesus, founded in 1540 by Ignacio Loyola and the most influential order in Spain for many centuries to come. As militant educational and spiritual leaders, the Jesuits placed themselves in the forefront of the ideological battle that raged in the Europe of the Counter-Reformation. Through their zeal, and armed with the weapon of the Inquisition, they were able to help Spain maintain her traditional religious fervor. It was Spain especially that personified the Counter-Reformation in the endeavor to fight the heresies of Protestanism. But after Spain lost her role as spiritual leader of

Europe, the Jesuits' role was retained only within the country itself. During this period of the late sixteenth and the seventeenth centuries, the intellectual life was stifled by an oppressive censorship. But despite this, arts and letters flourished sufficiently well to earn for the period the label of Spain's Golden Age. While Spain embraced religious fanaticism, the genius of her writers — like Lope de Vega and Calderón in the drama, Góngora in poetry, Cervantes and Quevedo in prose fiction, Gracián in aesthetics and moral philosophy, El Greco and Velázquez in painting — rose above an often oppressive and unstable society through artistic and philosophic expression.

Until relatively recently the seventeenth century has been considered by some critics an intensification of the Renaissance, whereas others see it as a decline. Regardless of these opposing attitudes the term *baroque* has become a label for the century; it is a term which covers a number of norms, philosophies, and literary conventions for not only Spain but all of Europe from about 1580 throughout approximately a century. Since the baroque in literature is fairly new, it is necessary to deal with its meaning, especially as it applies to Gracián, who, aside from exemplifying the baroque in his writings, composed the major aesthetic treatise of the century (see chapters 2 and 3).

Most scholars agree that the word is derived from *baroco*, which was used as a mnemonic term in logic. In the nineteenth century Jacob Burckhardt associated the baroque with the decadence of the High Renaissance, while Heinrich Wölfflin stabilized the term's meaning in his book *Renaissance und Barock*[3] by contrasting the two periods and applying Renaissance and baroque art categories of style to literature. Since Wölffin, there has been enormous interest in baroque as a positive concept, which has led to many ideas on the aesthetic significance of the period, its *Geist* and literary ideas.

III   *The Spanish Baroque*

As the seventeenth century progressed, a broad interpretation of reality was brought into prominence. The poet no longer only considered poetry in relation to the real world through its imitation of nature, but expanded the dimensions of reality into the realm of creation. That is, invention and creation provided the poet with a way to communicate truth. As opposed to the artist-artisan concept of the Renaissance writer, the baroque artist is an artist-inspirer. While the Renaissance writer stood *outside* his work, the baroque writer is wrapped within his creation, employing a very liberal artistic expression. Góngora's *Polyphemus* comes immediately to mind as an example of the author's involvement with chaotic nature contrasted to the idealized *loci amoeni* ("pleasant places") of Garcilaso's *Eclogues*. Also, the baroque artist distorts—some would say destroys — reality only to create a more abstract reality, such as is demonstrated in the apocalyptic and fantastic literature of the seventeenth century.[4]

Baroque literature is frequently a literature of ideas, thereby extensively displacing the Renaissance theory of art for art's sake.[5] Great tensions had not been resolved doctrinally in previous literary expressions; the artist, caught in a more chaotic and more complex life, expressed the polarities and tensions of existence. The baroque writer reflected the human condition in violent contrasts between lust and death, the temporal and the eternal, the sacred and the profane, appearance and reality. This is nowhere more evident than in the hyperbolic prose works of a Quevedo or of a Gracián. The baroque artist revealed his disturbed concern for the human situation by means of abnormal and intricate language, often apparently spontaneous yet ingenious in nature. Such writers as Donne, Marino, Góngora, Quevedo and Gracián shared this sensibility.

Many other characteristics define baroque aesthetics, and we will have occasion in chapter 3 to discuss Gracián's own theoretical contributions to its delineation. Baroque writers often attempted to fuse the genres into a kind of artistic catch-all, a *Gesamtkunstwerk*, in order to achieve a more dynamic and sophisticated effect. Cervantes's *Quixote* and Gracián's *The Master Critic* are good examples of this ideal and have often been described as a synthesis of many literary forms. Another baroque consideration is that mythology is not only enjoyed for its own sake, but is used to embroider and decorate literature, amplifying its grotesqueness and its beauty as well as its complexity. The *Solitudes* of Góngora exemplify this mythological embellishment.

In baroque writing one notes a new awareness of time; the poet-writer touches upon many aspects of time by means of his poetic structure — its relativity, its simultaneity, and its paradoxical nature. Thematic changes focus on the triumph of pessimism and cynicism over Renaissance humanistic idealism. There is little faith in a guiding concept of world harmony in the increasingly prominent attempt of the artist not only to debunk the organized view of reality of the sixteenth century but to substitute in its place an insistence on the irrational and the chaotic as common denominators of the human situation. It is therefore not surprising that one of the most significant contributions of the baroque is misanthropic satire and burlesque humor, which is often scatological. Giordano Bruno, Baltasar Gracián, and Francisco de Quevedo reflect such a view of man. Yet, one of the most outstanding contrasts of the baroque period is the coexistence of a literature of doubt and denial with the new rise in orthodox Christian expression and the religious literature of Tirso de Molina, Calderón de la Barca, and Torquato Tasso.

Besides the baroque aesthetic of creative imagination, spontaneity, and ingenuity, other characteristics describe baroque literature: the bizarre, the paradoxical, the extravagant, the grotesque, the horrible, the antithetic, the mutable, the dramatic, the elusive, the discordant. As for language in its effort to attain baroque ideals, the achievement came through an overwhelming intensification of dependence on the rhetorical figures of thought. Baroque literary language sought to develop a whole new range of verbal expression and experience, chiefly through the unrestrained practice of neologisms and the expression of verbal connotation. The realization of such a complex and intense language was achieved by the interaction of three dominant principles of baroque aesthetics: the conceit, extensive sensory and impressionistic imagery, and the use of *ingenio* ("imagination"). The most brilliant European writers to employ the baroque techniques are Góngora, Donne, Racine, Lope de Vega, Quevedo, and Marino. Gracián's aesthetic treatise, the *Agudeza y arte de ingenio* (The Mind's Wit and Art), is the first significant contemporary attempt to record those literary principles.

In the area of baroque art, Spain has produced the most brilliant poetry and literature of any European country. It is in Spain where the baroque movement is most closely identified as art of the Counter-Reformation, intensely national and fervently religious. Some critics consider Spain to be eternally baroque in literary expression, whereas others describe the baroque artistic expression as a reflection of the country's political crisis. Hence, especially in

Spain, a concern for "otherworldliness" and the "life-is-a-dream" concept are forcefully elaborated. The artist is an escapist, at least from a turbulent immediate reality, and to a degree there occurs a certain dehumanization of art. The works of Góngora, Quevedo, and Gracián demonstrate this attitude toward reality and unreality: all three describe flights from day-to-day values of their culture.

IV Rhetorical and Stylistic Schools

Discussion of Spanish baroque poetry usually centers around two groups of poets, those who practiced conceptism and those who practiced culteranism.[6] However, while it is superficially true that conceptism emphasizes the difficulty of thought and culteranism emphasizes the mechanics of language, the two groups are interrelated focal points of aesthetic practice rather than separate "schools." Both schools were concerned with the baroque aesthetic of *agudeza* ("wit") and the art of ingenio as elaborated by the major baroque preceptist, Baltasar Gracián. In the interest of analysis, however, conceptism gives greater significance to conciseness and brevity (cf. Gracián, "What is good, if brief, is twice as good"), clever concepts, wordplay, paradoxes, antithesis, and metaphors. On the other hand, culteranism sought an obscurity in style through neologisms, distorted syntax, hyperbole, and difficult allusions. A major literary battle was carried on between Quevedo and Góngora, the leaders of the two schools. Quevedo rejected Góngora's learned Latinization of Spanish and his hermetic expression, while the latter criticized Quevedo's puns, use of slang, intellectual conceits, and satiric humor. However, another factor in common between the two schools was their interest in the polysemous nature of words and literature.

It is, then, within this setting of history and ideas that one must place Gracián. His life and experience, nevertheless, differ somewhat from those of many of the Golden Age writers: he held no public office, received no special honors, and was a priest (a Jesuit), who spent his life in provincial posts as an educator. As a Jesuit, isolated to a certain extent in his religious Province of Aragón (which comprised Catalonia, Valencia, and Mallorca), he led two lives, that of a religious and that of an intellectual. As a religious, his rebel spirit was often tormented when he was forced to endure criticism and the rigid discipline of the order as well as its internal political strife.[7] As a sophisticated intellectual, he sought in his writings to impose upon what was still largely a medieval Spain a more up-to-date vision of man and society. He has earned the reputation of being the greatest of Spanish moral philosophers since Juan Vives, and only two of his six important works are non-moralistic: *El Comulgatorio* (The Communion Book), a guidebook to prayer, and the *Agudeza*, his work of literary criticism, which codifies those literary developments of his age that he was, from one point of view, so central to, and yet, from another, only a marginal observer of.

The Aesthetics of the Conceit: Gracián's Baroque Literary Doctrine in The Mind's Wit and Art

I *General Characteristics of* The Mind's Wit and Art.

I T has been frequently observed, virtually as a reader's lament, that the *Agudeza y arte de ingenio* (The Mind's Wit and Art) is an impossible work to follow because of its rambling and apparently unstructured exposition. Of course, such a lament derives from the modern reader's experience with contemporary criticism, which is based on the *sine qua non* of an expository format that adheres to an accepted methodology and organization for literary criticism. Obviously, such a methodology and organization cannot be demanded of Gracián retrospectively, and the most immediate task for a commentary on the *The Mind's Wit* is to disclose the pattern that does in fact underlie Gracián's treatise. Such a presentation is necessarily two-pronged: a general summary of what Gracián does talk about concerning wit and a synthetic analysis of the major literary topics of *The Mind's Wit* that can be extracted from the sprawl of his leisurely discourse.

When Gracián's manual of wit was published in definitive form in 1648 (a primitive version had appeared in 1642), the art of the conceit and wit were at an apogee of aesthetic importance for the seventeenth-century mind. This interest in conceptual relationships emphasized the rare, the unique, and the surprising by means of analogical extremes or opposites and likenesses; it was a "clever wit" that was held to effect such unexpected analogies. And wit came to be the source not only of intellectual pleasure but also of a moral instruction. In his treatise, the first two attempts define with copious examples all types of wit, Gracián analyzes wit as found in virtually all literary expression. According to Chambers,[1] herein lies the originality of the treatise: "Gracián's method brings together lyric poetry, epic poetry, oratory (in the form of sermons), prose fiction, history, biography, drama, the emblem, the parable, fable, the apologue, allegory, several varieties of wordplay, witty remarks and retorts, the epistle, moral philosophy, gestures, deeds and even conversation to prove that the mind and imagination, given the opportunity and a properly founded set of circumstances, can move them all into life by means of wit."

In his prologue to the reader, Gracián addresses himself to the importance of wit in literature:

I have devoted some of my works to discretion, and most recently my *Art of Prudence*, but this one I am dedicating to the Imagination—to wit in art, a resplendent conception—for even though some of its artifices glimmer in Rhetoric's discipline, still they hardly approach a sparkle: orphan children adopted by Eloquence, since they don't know their true mother. Wit makes use of rhetorical figures and tropes as devices for elegantly expressing its concepts; but they contain within their own limits the material foundations of nicety and, at best, the ornaments of thought. (p. 80; 230b)

In sixty-three *discursos* ("discourses"—chapters), Gracián defines, explains, and expounds upon wit. His treatise is divided into two parts: Discourses 1—50 are dedicated to the problem of simple wit, while thirteen chapters of the second part of the treatise discuss the complexities of compound wit. Both treatises abound in examples taken from biblical, classical, and seventeenth-century literature to support the literary opinions presented. Needless to say, Gracián's vast literary knowledge as seen through his facility to draw from a wide range of references gives the treatise more of a European than strictly Spanish dimension. The remainder of this chapter will detail what Gracián says about wit, whereas chapter 3 will give a presentation of the major literary ideas of *The Mind's Wit* which include Gracián's theory of poetry as intellectual play, drama, myth, and humor; his treatment of aspects of literary composition like style, erudition, good taste, and the ineffable; and his literary preferences and views on questions concerning baroque as a literary aesthetic.

Literature is by nature precedent to criticism, but it is criticism which places the reader in intimate intellectual contact with the works of literary creation upon which criticism is based or under whose influence it is written. When considering criticism in the seventeenth century, one is apt to think of such distinguished writers as Boileau, Tesanno, Lope de Vega, and Ben Jonson. Although many critics have praised and studied the works of Baltasar Gracián no one has attempted to investigate in detail the development of his critical and literary ideas. This chapter undertakes to do this, placing special emphasis on those literary problems that interested Gracián: imitation versus creation, truth, reality, imagination, and the nature of poetry, *agudeza* ("wit"), *buen gusto* ("good taste"), and *no sé qué* ("*je ne sais quoi*"; the ineffable). Gifted with a perceptive mentality, Gracián has shared many ideas with critics of all ages who have probed the essence of literature and its problems. His contributions to the main currents of literary expression through analyses of the literary practices of his age and his original theory of literature reveal intelligent insights into the baroque and constitute a fundamental part of Spanish and European literary theory of the seventeenth century. This presentation, therefore, attempts to evaluate Baltasar Gracián as a literary critic and to underline the transcendental nature of his critical doctrine in *The Mind's Wit and Art.*

II   *Initial Definitions of Wit*

The Mind's Wit, written in a direct style and panegyric tone, is a unique and interesting treatise in the Western literary tradition. Given the fact that much literary criticism, especially in Spain, has been an aggressive defense of particular literary taste[2] and a means for correcting the writers' art, it is refreshing to read Gracián's work, in which no literary movements or ideas are condemned. Instead, Gracián first points out opposing literary opinions and then, with an abundance of examples, proceeds to emphasize his own literary ideas and preferences. The position of superiority occupied by *The Mind's Wit* in European letters rests on many factors: it introduces a new central concept into aesthetic theory through the careful examination of every kind of agudeza and conceit within a broad universal context of literature; it offers many insights into imaginative literature, both profane and sacred; it expresses many informative opinions on the significance and craft of writing; it exemplifies baroque aesthetics and provides a justification for the nature of metaphysical poetry and hermetic expression. Moreover, *The Mind's Wit,* the *tour de force* of Hispanic literary criticism, stresses two vital aspects of literature—intellectual beauty and didacticism—and establishes a principle that is later elaborated in *The Master Critic* (see chapter 5): man may be saved from mediocrity and a deceitful world by means of literature and art. As Curtius has remarked, the work is an intellectual achievement of high rank, a *Summa* of agudeza.[3]

The complete title *Agudeza y arte de ingenio en que se explican todos los modos y diferencias de conceptos,* (Wit and Art of Ingenuity, in Which are Explained all Manner and Differences of Conceits),[4] brings together three related concepts: agudeza, ingenio, and *concepto* ("conceit"). Gracián's basic theories rest within the framework of these terms of complex connotations. Therefore, the best means of capturing the essence of these concepts is to give a view of the interpretations advanced by various scholars (the translations are mine):

Agudeza for him is the only source of esthetic pleasure, a generic notion which takes in all perfections and beauties of style. *Agudeza* for Gracián is a synonym of literary beauty.[5]

"Keenness," *agudeza,* is to be taken as intellectual sharpness or in a more exact but unsympathetic English equivalent: "smartness." "The mind's art" is this keenness or smartness, and it seems therefore implied that such keenness is the function of the mind. Gracián's object then is to expound intellectual activity. The ambiguity lies in the word *agudeza* which can be either the equivalent of *ingenio,* wit, a function of a subdivision of understanding or else one synonym of *concepto.*[6]

Agudeza is the "faculty of acuteness."[7]

Wit *(agudeza)* is not at all an "intellectual" act in any merely descriptive sense, but is the work of the understanding functioning artistically. It is quite reasonable for him to use the term *agudeza* in the second part of the work to embrace, in a larger sense, all imaginative literature.[8]

Wit *(agudeza),* then, is to be assessed finally, not in the validity of the argument involved, or even in the verbal graces with which it is adorned, but in the beauty which, as we have seen, being perceived by the understanding as it contemplates the ordered art of nature, has been expressed in the conceit.[9]

Agudeza is often called *concept,* after the fashion of the *conceptistas* [writers of conceits] of the time.[10]

Gracián never gives a generally valid definition of *agudeza.* It is possible to infer its meaning from the different places dealing with the particular varieties of *agudeza* (outcome) and clarify it from the related concepts (meaning) [brought out] from different perspectives. Thus perhaps as in the previously cited case of "subtlety of ingenuity" plus "art."[11]

The relationship of *ingenio* and *agudeza* refers exclusively to the wit of artifice, that is, to wit that is oriented in terms of beauty and not to wit oriented in terms of truth.[12]

Agudeza is wit. The term is not specifically defined, but its synonyms help to fix its meaning: *sutileza, prontitud, gracia, donosidad.*[13]

Gracián himself, although inconsistent in the use of the term, provides insights into the nature of wit (agudeza) when he refers to its four ingredients:

Devices of wit serve as the recreation of the soul, and though they may not astonish, they do delight; a happy turn of phrase in a letter is like an enigma in a sermon, and a sudden witticism in conversation is as delightful as a maxim in a Papal consistory, for if a star may sparkle in the most exalted part of heaven, a flower may spring up as well in the lowliest reach of a valley. (pp. 863—64; 498a)

Elegant polish, difficulty, and conciseness are associated with the term agudeza in Gracián's interpretation. Whether the word "agudeza" is best defined as the "faculty of acuteness" or as the creative faculty of the writer, one observes that such mental keenness is of paramount importance in the literary act; agudeza associated with ingenio, therefore encompasses the ability of the writer to think ingeniously and to create the most hidden, unique, similar, and dissimilar conceits.

"Ingenio," also an equivocal word which is, at times, associated with sensibility, imagination, understanding and creative talent.

Maldonado de Guevara has pointed out the Renaissance liberal interpretation of this word, that constitutes "todo el fondo del Ser" (the whole depth of Being), intellectually, morally, and artistically.[14] Words which in Gracián accompany "ingenio" include *agudo* ("sharp"), *famoso* ("famous"), *sabio* ("wise"), *inventivo* ("inventive"), *admirable* ("admirable"), *incomparable* ("incomparable"), *valiente* ("valiant"), *renombrado* ("renowned"), *inspiración* ("inspiration"). Gracián advances an original interpretation of the term "ingenio" by designating it as the imaginative or inventive faculty of the writer. Since various critics have discussed the meaning of "ingenio,"[15] a survey of the term is in order for added clarity:

'Judgment' ("juicio") is satisfied with truth, whereas understanding ("ingenio") [is satisfied] with beauty (beauty here is 'agudeza').[16]

Gracián's term "arte de ingenio" gives the clue for historical comprehension. We must go back to classical rhetoric . . . *Ingenium*, then, belongs in the realm of *inventio*. But a genius for clever invention degenerates into a fault if it is not coupled with judgment.

How is the relation between *ingenium* and *iudicium* defined? This question was discussed by Spanish theorists in the sixteenth century. Juan de Valdés shows that it lies with the judgment to choose the best from among the stock of the *ingenium* and to put it in its proper place; "invention" and "disposition" are the two principal parts of rhetoric; the former corresponds to the *ingenio*, the latter to *juicio*. This is the linguistic usage from which Gracián also sets out.[27]

In the general discussion of wit with which *The Mind's Wit* begins, the term *ingenio*, which is not formally defined, is used to mean the understanding *(entendimiento)* in its function of producing wit.[18]

"Genio" is that which is static in man; "ingenio," that which is dynamic: rest and motion, the two poles of life.

An additional significant attribute of ingenuity is the rapidity and agility of thought, the swift grasping of a circumstance, the quick-witted or prompt repartee. Gracián denotes this with the word *prontiutud* ["promptness"], occasionally with *presteza* ["quickness"] or with *viveza de ingenio* ["liveliness of ingenuity"] (the latter being like one of the definitions in the *Diccionario de autoridades* [Dictionary of authorities]).[19]

"Ingenio" is that human faculty from which is derived "agudeza" and the one which in the last Discourse of *The Mind's Wit* acts as the principal cause of "agudeza." Hence an explanation that "ingenio"—as opposed to judiciousness—can be related, rather than . . . with what is real, with what is possible, what is fictitious.[20]

Ingenio. Here imagination, but elsewhere often translated as mind, talent . . . It is also used in reference to the degree of effectiveness of thought and expression, of the success with which man rationalizes and expounds (as opposed to the connotations of *genio*, the potential that man has before any use is made of it). Thus the adjective *ingenioso* is often rendered *ingenious, clever* or *talented*, but with Gracián never carries notions of superficial facileness.[21]

Gracián offers insights into the word "ingenio" and like Aristotle, he considers imagination to be the highest faculty of the mind. Gracián states that ingenio is the most forceful cause of wit, and he ultimately bases his entire theory of literature on ingenio.

In Gracián's theory the exercise of wit and ingenuity is expressed by the conceit, the concepto, that is, the profound conceptual idea. In his opinion the conceit is a thought process as well as a rhetorical device which enabled contemporary writers to surpass the ancient masters; the conceit corrected the defects of nature through the expression of a correspondence between concrete or abstract ideas. Essentially, Gracián's doctrine is a poetic of correspondences; he is the first theorist to initiate and define for Spain a poetic of the conceit on the basis that the artistic form of the conceit reveals truth, varying aspects of human experience and delightful harmonies and contrasts. Several critics in particular, have made important contributions to an understanding of Gracián's theory:

Although it is true that Gracián is not so consistent as we could wish, there does seem to be a definite tendency to take *agudeza* as the faculty, and *concepto* as the exemplification, the individual result of "mental keenness."[22]

His most striking originality lies in his doctrine of the intellectual *concepto*, that is to say, in his idea of the conceit as a single special act of the understanding.[23]

The different representations joined in metaphor were, for the universally acknowledged father of the new movement, two "knowable extremes," while its faculty capable of binding them was "ingegno" or "wit." In binding extremes, the "ingegno" produced a metaphor or conceit.[24]

The concept . . . is in a certain sense a formal figure, allowing us to move conceits from one level to another, a difficulty of definition before which Gracián at times finds himself. The conceit thus expresses the *stylistic* reality which in general is based on the *esthetic reality*.[25]

That is to say, one could understand that, for Gracián, the conceit is purely a game of intelligence, the product of an intellect put in tension and stretched to its limit, with the goal of achieving the most violent association of ideas. "Agudeza" would then be something like an exquisite liquor, an elixir, a quintessence, arrived at by cerebral pressure and effort placed at the service of poetry.[26]

The conceit, then, consists of an agreeable relation between two or more knowable extremes, expressed by the understanding . . . Comparisions are drawn, terms are brought face to face, the subject with its adjuncts or the adjuncts among themselves, until a suitable relationship is found and worked into the context.[27]

In the sixty-three Discursos of his guidebook for poets and writers Gracián discusses extensively simple and compound conceptos, the nature of style, and many other literary ideas. In general, one may view his theory in the following manner: wit and/or insight (agudeza) aided by the imagination (ingenio) are the requisites for creating conceptos that embrace the complex relationships in literary expression by means of multiple literary forms and devices.

III An Analytical Classification of the
Forms of Conceit in The Mind's Wit

Gracián's discursive presentation of his descriptive evaluation of the various types of wit and conceits may be defined in baroque terminology as dispersion and conversion, respectively. The haphazard system of his exposition diverges in several directions, which nevertheless converge on the constant point of agudeza. Thus, Gracián divorces himself from the classical procedure of rhetoric and logic in order to present his ideas in his own personal, ingenious way. He writes an *arte de ingenio y agudeza* that is exhaustive,

often pedantic, and a bit chaotic. An organizational framework underlying Gracián's disorderly presentation may nevertheless be
demonstrated.[28]

His first fifty discourses discuss the general and specific nature of
agudeza incompleja, ("simple wit") the veritable basis of the entire
treatise. However, the general considerations of *agudeza* are
contained in Discourses 1—3, and on these general considerations
Gracián bases his study of the more specific forms of simple wit and
the conceit (see sections 4—7 below). These are the main lines of his
broad classifications of simple wit:

1) *Agudeza de perspicacia* ("wit via perspicaciousness"): wit
which expresses truth. This type of agudeza is a useful and fresh
adjunct to all the arts and sciences.

2) *Agudeza de artificio* ("wit via artifice"): the delightful,
abstract, and artistic form of wit, most highly favored and
extensively developed in the treatise. Its finer components are:

a) *Agudeza de conceptos* ("wit via conceits"): wit which
concentrates on the subtlety of the thought rather than on the
word.

b) *Agudeza verbal* ("verbal wit"): wit deriving from puns
and play on words.

c) *Agudeza de acción* ("wit via action"): wit through clever
and contrived actions.

3) *Agudeza de correspondencia* ("wit via correspondences"):
wit found in comparisons.

4) *Agudeza de contrariedad* ("wit via opposites"): wit produced by antithetical figures of speech.

5) *Agudeza pura* ("pure wit"): wit with only one subtle idea.

6) *Agudeza mixta* ("mixed wit"): wit in a type of conceit which
contains three or four subtle thoughts.

7) *Agudeza incompleja* ("simple wit"): wit attained by two or
three witty devices within a simple conceit like an epigram or a
sonnet. (Lest the reader be confused, we repeat that *agudeza
incompleja* is given as one form of wit in Discourses 1—3,
although thereafter the bulk of the treatise is an elaboration of
this one, basic form of wit.)

8) *Agudeza compuesta* ("compound wit"): wit found in a series
of simple conceits, or in an extended metaphor or in some fiction
like an epic poem or an allegory.

Gracián does not complete his discussion of *agudeza* until Discourse 43, the last chapter of the treatise. Here, the four sources of wit are seen to lie in (1) imagination, (2) invention, (3) imitation of the best of the ancient literary works, and (4) art in general. These sources of agudeza are summarized in a general survey of the possibilities of wit based on a fourfold classification of agudeza incompleja proposed by Gracián and based on correlation, ponderation, ratiocination, and invention. This scheme, more than any other, marks Gracián's more specific attitudes toward his subject.

IV   *Wit by Correlation*

As just seen, wit by correlation is one of the classifications of simple wit that is achieved by means of comparisons and contrasts. Discourses, 4, 5, 9—20, 31—34, 44, 68, 69 concentrate on this classification. The fundamental principle of the modes of conceit and wit in the correlative category may be grouped as follows.

1. Agudeza by Comparisons

Comparison is the most obvious aspect of wit; Gracián confirms its intrinsic worth in a wide variety of literary forms, such as in an epithet of Petrarch, a couple of sonnets of Góngora and Guarini, and an epigram of Martial.[29] He believes that all clever writers find a relationship between widely divergent ideas. In addition, those conceits involving proportional relationships reflect an intellectual symmetry of ideas as portrayed in a sonnet by Francisco de la Cueva, which Gracián analyzes. Comparisons, therefore, develop their full meaning only in the medium of agudeza.

Another source for witty conceits is the simile, which is not strictly a rhetorical device in Gracián's aesthetics. The simile is an art form because it is a product of the imaginative faculty, ingenio. Discourse 9 discusses the similitude or simile as the "tercer principio de agudeza sin límite" ("third principle of boundless wit"). Although even the simplest similes contain beautiful ideas, what Gracián warmly defends is the accumulation of similes, such as we find in an elegiac *canción* ("song") by Quevedo. Most important is that the *semejanza* ("similarity") may be inventive or intuitive. The correspondence is not always real. A good example, according to Gracián, is Horace's *Ars poetica*, in which a monstrous animal or being is likened to the works of some writers.

Still another type of wit is found in the paradoxical simile. The artist achieves striking effects of contrast and proportion by means of two juxtaposed similes. Such wit is defended in Discourse 10. Quevedo's ballad "De Dafne y Apolo" (On Daphne and Apollo), Marino's madrigal "Del Nascimento de Christo" (On the Birth of Christ), and Góngora's sonnet to San Ignacio are examples of works that use the paradoxical simile. Paradox for Gracián is the height of artistic and intellectual subtlety.

Enigma and difficulty are two vital requisites for the poet's art. In Discourse 40 Gracián expresses his theory of difficulty with reference to the complicated and enigmatic simile; the greater the complication, the more brilliant the simile. Special ways for the artist to achieve this complexity of wit lie in the artist's reference to names and events in the literary work. The *Panegiri* of the historian Pliny, a sonnet by Luis Carrillo called "El primer culto de España" ('Spain's first learned [poet]'), and an epigram by Martial are cited as examples of difficulty based on enigma. The designation of the moral simile as an unusually effective source of wit fits within Gracián's doctrine that all literature has a moral mission. In Discourse 12 the *semejanza sentenciosa* ("sententious similarity"), which extracts "una moralidad provechosa" ("a useful morality"), echoes the Horatian doctrine of *dulce et utile*. Gracián states that this type of simile requires much *arte de ingenio* in that the artistic transformation of events and personal experience conveys excellent moral ideas. The literary devices that enrich the simile are satire and "la gustosa crisi" ("the pleasing *crisi*"), a kind of moral censure.[30] Those artists who include the moral simile in their craft are Lope de Vega, the learned Italian poet and historian Pontano Joviano, and Alciato in his emblematic literature, which depends on the reader's experiencing a visual conceit.[31]

2. Agudeza by Contrasts

In Discourse 5 one learns that a juxtaposition of contrary terms can lead to wit. Great conceits are produced from the *correlación de contrariedad* ("correlation by contraries"), which is in Gracián's opinion a type of literary perfection. "La luz mirando con la luz ciega" ("Light seeing with blind light") from the conceit of Juan de Valdés exemplifies the practice of inverting thoughts. This art of creating dissimilar analogies is a particular talent of Spanish writers. Most of Gracián's examples center on Spanish poets, such as Fray Luis de León, Francisco de la Torre, Bartolomé Leonardo Argensola, Lope de Vega, Góngora, and others. Gracián also suggests a method for effecting contrasts: the poet may find pointed contrasts in the effects of certain emotions (e.g., profane love), or in the juxtaposition of incongruous terms (i.e., oxymoron) as in the phrase "capricious fortune," where an adjective and noun not usually associated together are employed.

Discourse 13 amplifies Gracián's doctrine of contrasts advanced in Discourse 5. The question at hand focuses on conceits by dissimilarities, the poetical presentation of ideas by showing the dissimilarity between two phenomena, such as immutable nature and ephemeral man. St. Ambrose and Góngora are the artists of ingenio who excel in the use of *desemejanza* ("dissimilarity"). The forms best suited for this category are: sonnet, panegyric, epigram, sermon, emblem, *crisi*, and the riddle.

Contrasts are best achieved by paradox, one of Gracián's favorite literary devices, which is treated in Discourse 23. Paradoxes are "monstruos de la verdad" ("monsters of truth"), because they are structured on mere opinion and not truth. Therefore, the poet must be prudent in using the paradox, for no writer has succeeded solely through his use of paradoxical expression. Nevertheless, the competent writer may contrive ingenious paradoxes to form subtle and inventive conceits that provide intellectual pleasure and moral profit. Paradox is a flexible and popular form of expression among historians, preachers, and natural philosophers, as well as writers of fiction. Gracián refers to Luis Vélez de Guevara, who communicated instantaneous wit in a ballad, to Seneca in his adages, and to Don Juan Manuel in his delightful tales.[32]

3. Agudeza and Rhetoric

Although Gracián denies any reliance on rhetoric, he is in fact heavily dependent on it.[33] This point is clearly evident in Discourses 31 and 48 in the discussions of wit based on the clever use of nouns as a source for richness of style as well as for an erudite type of wit and conceit. This referential technique is of particular vitality in sermons (of Fray Reimundo Gracián and Padre Felipe Gracián, for example), in religious poetry (e.g., that of Marino, Francisco Andrés de Uztarroz, and Manuel de Salinas), and in the secular art of Martial, Góngora, and Guarini. Gracián enthusiastically suggests that the poet employ paranomasia, two words juxtaposed, one spelled backward from the other, such as *Roma-amor* ("Rome-love"), which suggests the former as the center of profane love by juxtaposing phenomenon and locale. The use of cryptic or unfamiliar names is another way to practice clever wit. Epithets and satirical nicknames and puns give life to words, lead to profound ideas, and delight the reader. Among those writers who use nominal wit are Quevedo, Góngora, and Alciato.

Another device, that of allusion, complements Gracián's doctrine of hermetic and erudite expression. The discussion in Discourse 49 shows how allusion, a sublime and enigmatic device, injects wit and ingenuity into various examples of literary expression. Allusion to some historical or mythological event, person, place, saying, or thing intensifies the conceit; its great artistry lies in its power of suggestion, which entertains the intellectual aristocracy and provokes curiosity among the uninformed masses. Suetonius, Martial, Antonio de Mendoza, Góngora, and Lope are especially skillful and erudite writers who appreciate this highly praised device.

4. Agudeza by Overall Structural Devices

Gracián's theory of artistic wit includes the consideration of literature in architectural terms; our critic frequently describes the symmetry, harmony, balance, and beauty of literary expression. Both the intellectual and visual imagery of a poem or prose work are considered in his study. One way to effect a type of wit with architectural characteristics is by parallel structure. Discourse 17 energetically defends the sustained device based on comparative or antithetical terms, such as we might find in a sonnet where one series of phenomena (e.g., aspects of nature) is juxtaposed to another, parallel series of phenomena (e.g., the features of a woman's body). A strong allegiance to his native Aragón incites Gracián to refer to the artistry of many Aragonese writers who employ this parallel device: Martial; Bartolomé Leonardo de Argensola, who was called "aquel gran filósofo en verso" ("that great philosopher in verse"); the historians Juan Francisco Andrés de Uztarroz and Jerónimo Zurita; and the sermonizer Fray Gabriel Hernández.[34]

Another artistic form of poetic license is textual accommodation, which establishes a figurative relationship between series of biblical or classical persons, objects, or events (and thereby a new truth) and requires an intense conceptual power on the part of the writer as well as the reader (Discourse 34). Agudeza in this class, therefore, is oriented along intellectual lines by any writer who exercises poetic license. Gracián recommends that a well-known text be accommodated in a very liberal fashion by changing the text or adding to it. The sermon is the genre best suited for accommodation. Padre Juan Aznola, a contemporary Jesuit friend of Gracián's; Sebastián de Barradas; Francisco Suárez; Bernardino de Villegas; Pedro de Valderrama; and other Jesuits are cited for their contributions in their notable and witty conceits in the art of accommodating texts in sermons.

5. Agudeza by Affective Devices

In the preceding pages an inquiry into the serious and sublime aspects of agudeza has been made. In the treatise one finds an abundance of references in which Gracián prescribes an affective approach to literary creation. Consequently, a clever, popular type of wit, *agudeza picante* ("piquant, biting wit"), is formed from the extraordinary use of language and ideas. The spirit of the conceit is light, jocular, burlesque that is often satirical. Gracián is very enthusiastic about affective wit and exaggerated conceits, and therefore he is frequently repetitive in the presentation of his ideas on them.

Discourse 17 discusses one of the most delightful types of conceits wherein artistic and inventive wit is created by transforming an object into the contrary of what it seems to be. This method is labeled that of *ingeniosas trasposiciones* ("ingenious transpositions"). Jorge de Montemayor turned happiness to grief in a canción; Alciato converted a place into a prison, but Traiano Boccalini is unsurpassed in his inventive talent for criticizing society in a challenging and unexpected way.

Two Discourses, 29 and 20, further demonstrate Gracián's unflagging and insistent praise of burlesque wit based on overstatement and hyperbole. The device of overstatement brings the concept of the marvelous and the fantastic into literary expression. Gracián readily accepts this *género de sutileza* ("genre of subtlety"), which is best portrayed by satire, exaggerated antithesis, eulogy, and mystery. Horace, Martial, Jaime Juan Falcón, called "el Marcial de Valencia" ("Valencia's Martial"), Góngora, and Lope de Vega figure in this type of wit involved in overstatement. Discourse 20 justifies the hyperbole for its sensitive and marvelous conceits based on quandaries, adages, puzzles, and difficult and exaggerated ideas. Hyperbolic writing appears especially in the *apothegmas* ("maxims") of Juan Rufo, the poetry of Lope and Góngora, the sermons of Baltasar's brother Felipe Gracián, and in the *ragguagli* ("reports") of Bocccalini.

There is still another analysis of wit derived from affective devices: suspense and surprise. This type of conceit predominates in Discourse 44, in which Gracián praises the building of tension with unfulfilled release, typical of seventeenth-century literary expression. Those artists most skillful in wit by suspense and surprise include Camões in his love poetry, Góngora and Quevedo in their burlesque poetry, and Lope de Vega in his *Rimas humanas* (Human Rhymes).

V *Wit by Ponderation*

Ponderación ("ponderation"), the second broad classification, offers another set of perspectives on agudeza. Through the discussions of Discourses 6—8, 26—30, 43, and 46, further qualities of the conceit emerge: criticism, obscure truth, contradiction, and enigma. The term "ponderation" denotes surprise, wonder, and perplexity — all phenomena dear to the seventeenth-century mind. Ponderation requires strenuous mental effort to grasp the meaning of the two relationships in the conceit; the art form of the conceit now reflects a difficult reality in that the explanatory part of the conceit does not constitute a satisfactory relationship to the introductory segment of the conceit. The procedure is indirect, based on abstract and sophisticated insights, and therefore the resulting agudeza is more subtle than the agudeza of the correlative mode. It is possible to consider *la agudeza por ponderación* from the following points of view.

1. Agudeza by Admiration (Wonderment)[35]

Discourses 6—8 evaluate the various methods (curiosity, admiration, or awe) for inciting ponderation in the literary work. Mystery by means of hints and concealed explanations is a way to attain subtle wit and the marvelous. Gracián justifies the device of mystery on the basis of its universality and flexibility as used in religious, political, historical, and artistic writings such as in those works of St. Matthew, Velleius Paterculus, Pliny, Alciato, Camões, Góngora, and Lope de Vega. Difficult and hermetic expression increases the degree of wonder and perplexity in the conceit. Exaggeration, difficult relationships, contrasts, and parallels are effective devices. The religious themes of religious and secular artists illustrate particularly well the art of complicated expression. The practice of citing religious examples of poetry and prose seems to indicate the effect of the *Ratio Studiorum*[36] on our Jesuit critic. St. Thomas Aquinas, Pedro de Salazar, Lucian, Marino, and Lope de Vega are only a few of the writers who portray difficult art in their treatment of religious subjects. *Admiratio*, this wonderment to be awakened in the reader by the author's wit, resides in wit through ponderation, for contradictions of terms challenge the mind with their subtlety and invention. Paradox, antithesis, erudition, and allusions should constitute part of the artist's resources. The best example of this type of wit is Christ himself, who spoke in contradictory terms: "Novi et aeterni testamenti" ("a new and eternal testament").

2. Agudeza by Sententiousness[37]

In this category, caustic wit intensifies the *dulce et utile* aesthetic of Gracián's theory. Discourse 26 develops caustic wit as a superior facet of *conceptismo* ("the use of conceits") in that the ingenio forces practical ideas by means of crisi, sermon, epigram, or by other forms of poetry. Furthermore, the sententious wit of Discourse 29, born of the artist's prudence and imagination, represents the apex of wit. Maxims incorporated within the artistic work of prose or poetry result in an instructive and pleasurable literature.

Skillful sententious wit is also created by means of the derisive crisi discussed in Discourse 17. While caustic wit censures human shrewdness, sententious wit satirizes human limitations. Gracián cites his patron's brother, Juan Orencio de Lastanosa, for this type of ingenious wit. Another class of profound wit is portrayed in the prudent crisi (Discourse 18), in which criticism is subtly suggested rather than stated. Again faithful to his native Aragón, Gracián refers to the prudent remarks and profound wit of Pablo de Parada,[38] called "el Cid de nuestros tiempos" ("the Cid of our times"), as well as to the fables and allegories of Mateo Alemán in his *Guzmán de Alfarache*.

Discourse 30 on heroic proverbs, Discourse 43 on prudent maxims, and Discourse 44 on heroic sayings deal with categories of agudeza by *sententia* ("sententiousness"). Useful truth is derived from this type of conceit, which is highly praised by Gracián. He makes interesting distinctions when he says that heroic proverbs are oriented toward the sentiments of virtue, maxims venture into intellectual profundities, and heroic sayings immortalize the spontaneous ingenio of famous men.

VI *Wit by Ratiocination*

It is particularly interesting to follow Gracián presentation in the third category of wit, which he places in the realm of ratiocination. Discourses 36—42 summarize the intellectual type of conceit, which is contrived by the process of exact reasoning, either inductively or deductively. Again, Gracián's orientation toward logic as a basis of literary expression reflects his identification with the *Ratio Studiorum*. Agudeza now may be divided into two categories, agudeza by arguments and agudeza by *sutileza* ("subtlety").

1. Agudeza by Arguments

Discourses 36 and 46 develop the many dimensions that argument as a procedure may take in the work of literature. The argumentative part of the poem or prose work has value in that arguments intensify emotions, thereby causing an emotional response to take place within the reader. For instance, a poet like Guarini links the images in his poem by a logical thread of argumentative thought in order to produce wit. Gracián follows a traditional view of argument and applies rhetorical terms to the methods of conceitful arguments. *Ab exemplo*, "arguments by use of examples," or *a repugnantibus*, "arguments by contradiction of the contrary," represent two of the various methods.

2. Agudeza by Sutileza

A fundamental aspect of wit is its subtlety compounded with spontaneity and ingenuity. The Spanish writers are particularly gifted with this talent. Wit through the device of inference forms a good conceit. Although Gracián prescribes inference by use of paradox and contradiction in Discourse 38, he states that no certain rules can be applied to attain this form of wit born of extraordinary sutileza. That is, more ingenuity than simply technical skill is required in order to reveal unexpected truths by inference. The most outstanding technicians of this poetic device are Fray Luis de León and Bartolomé Leandro de Argensola.

Discourses 39 and 41 pursue further the art of subtlety and wit through riddles and ingenious questions that challenge the reasoning powers of the reader. Gracián believes that questions are a clever way to begin a work; for example, Horace began his satires with a question. The critic's brother, Felipe Gracián, excels in the use of moral and didactic riddles in sermons. Problematic questions with no solutions and riddles oriented toward a strict moral purpose are intellectual conceits which contain a high degree of sutileza and wit. Discourse 41 studies briefly the sutileza of quick replies. This device reinforces Gracián's doctrine of brevity and spontaneity of expression, and Martial and Laertius Diogenes are cited.

Enigmatic wit is another manifestation of sutileza in the literary work. Discourse 40 discusses how a fact or a great emotion can be transformed into artistic terms by means of contradictory statements, riddles, and difficult questions so as to produce an enigma. Garcilaso de la Vega offers a typical example of this enigmatic approach when he poetically defines jealousy in a sonnet.

Sutileza is further evident in the poetic expression in the contradicton of emotions and passions. This device is the concern of Discourse 42, in which this type of conceit is shown to be exclusively evident in the art of poetry. Gracián favors the recreation of intense emotional experience by means of poetic writing. Therefore, an art which relies on the play of emotions has both agudeza and sutileza. Such is the *conceptista* poetry of Gabriel Bocángel, Luis de Góngora, and Antonio de Mendoza.

VII *Wit by Invention*

The fourth broad classification, *invención* ("invention"), covered in Discourses 25, 45 and 47, reveals Gracián's unique orientation in Spanish seventeenth-century literary theory. The Jesuit's most striking contributions are his insistence upon original literary expression based on creation and upon drawing parallels between life and literature. Although the *Criticón* is his one work that most extensively elaborates the latter point (see chapter 5), the *Agudeza* manifests some early ideas on the subject. Wit by invención not only stresses creation but also draws the analogy between life and literature in the following ways.

1. Agudeza by Remarks

Sayings constitute magnificent conceits within a poem or within a work of literature, and this form of spontaneous invention is the subject of Discourse 25. Gracián substantiates his point by reference to the striking observations of life made by his uncle Antonio Gracián regarding the virtue of the stubborn nature of the Aragonese temperament.

2. Agudeza by Striking Deeds

In Discourse 45 the chaotic and exciting events of mythology, history and life are suggested as rich sources for imaginative literature. Life and truth are mirrored particularly in the involved plots and complex intrigues of the myths. A good example of this practice is to be found in the genius of the Spanish national theater, which Gracián defends, although he thinks that the Italian Guarini's *Pastor Fido*[39] is the apex of dramatic genius. However, he praises the ingenious intrigues of Lope, Guillén de Castro, and Calderón as well as the prose works of Apuleius, Heliodorus, and John Barclay, who artistically recorded great deeds and lives. The customs of life inspire imaginative literary expression, and Discourse 47 dwells on how man's actions and heroic deeds may be immortalized by the work of art. Gracián emphasizes the clever actions of strategy, a true art of life, which has inspired painting as well as literary creation, as for example, the original strategem of Hypericles, which was immortalized by Plutarch.

The profile of simple wit drawn in Part I of the treatise is perfected by Gracián's study of complex wit in Part II. Although thirteen *discursos* constitute the "segundo tratado," Gracián gives only a brief analysis of complex or compound wit. Compound wit essentially embraces all forms of simple wit, with an increased intensity in the breadth and depth of the conceptual artifice. Therefore, Gracián continues to see all literary forms as conceits whether they are epics, fables, apologues, or sermons. The Aragonese *preceptista* ("literary theoretician, preceptist") elaborates on two modes of compound wit:

> Compound wit exists in two modes, and there are two species of compounds. The first species is that which is composed of simple conceits, such as three or four proportions, three or four quandaries, parallels, et cetera, unified among themselves, which make their play through correspondence. The second is a compound by means of fiction, such as epics, continued allegories, dialogues, etc. (p. 767; 461b)

The conclusion that is drawn from the foregoing analysis is that wit is found in all forms of literary expression but most prominently in poetry, since poetry is the genre of imaginative writing that best substantiates Gracián's general theory of a literature of difficult and original expression based on agudeza, ingenio, and concepto.

CHAPTER 3

The Concept of Poetry in The Mind's Wit and Art

Introduction: Toward a Definition of Poetry

THE concept of *verdad poética* ("poetic truth") that appears in *The Mind's Wit* represents a significant departure from the seventeenth-century Spanish concept of Christian truth, as based on the Bible. For Gracián there are many kinds of truth, and the poet, by means of agudeza and ingenio, can present not only the mimetic truth which derives from the imitation of nature but, by means of the concepto, brings out the nonobvious but more profound truth of life and is successful in making things that are not, appear to be. As Curtius explains,[1] Gracián favors truth drawn on the synthesis of *prodesse* and *delectare:* imaginative poetry creates a kind of truth which both instructs and delights the reader.

Gracián maintains that the best ancient and modern poets resorted to the aesthetic of the *dulce engañar* ("sweet deceit") in order to convey truth, because *la verdad desnuda* ("naked truth") is ugly, bitter, and unconvincing.[2] The Jesuit subordinates truth to wit, illustrating his position by relating an allegory in which wit saves truth from *mentira,* "lie" (cf. the *Obras completas,* pp. 473 a/b). It is wit that enhances and fortifies moral and philosophic truths which have been artistically expressed. Moreover, Gracián advances the idea that truth and reality have many perspectives: "one truth may be dressed in many ways" (p. 802; 473b).

Another defense of poetic truth is found in the Jesuit's quotation of Boccalini's defense of the inventions and deceits of poets on the basis that they tell possible truths. Apollo had ordered the poets to sing in their verses only of proven truths produced in nature. The poets rebelled:

> Upon hearing this, the poets rose up and began to complain harshly that Apollo should bother with forbidding their learned and clever inventions during an age of lies — that was to steal the soul from poetry! — and not consider the fact that the most learned men of Parnassus, politicians as well as historians, have always received eulogistic encomiums for announcing as true numberless things that have been neither seen nor heard of among men, such as the idea that there are disinterested human beings, men who prefer public advantage to private interest, ministers who are not slaves of their passions, princes free of ambition and the audacity of desiring the possessions of others, men of integrity, heroes, universal men, etc. (p. 340; 319b)

To be sure, Gracián was able to agree that not all poetic truth springs from impeccable sources. In an explanation of mysterious wit, paraphrasing an anonymous and erudite humanist, he complains about the sensual nature of poetry, "because poets are ordinarily impious hacks of lasciviousness" (p. 178; 265a).

Poetry and literature in general are not restricted to true statements, but include fiction, what ought to be, what is true and real, the false, and mere opinion. What is more, the poet is urged to "create what cannot be," thereby elevating *la verdad poética* ("poetic truth") from the realm of the probable, lifelike, and likely to the realm of the fantastic:

> It is but a small thing to reason on the possible if one can never rise above it toward the impossible. The other species of wit indicate what is, this one what might be; nor is it content with this, but flings itself toward the contrary — toward what cannot be. (p. 347; 321 a/b)

Poetic truth raises three issues of poetry: imagination, invention, and imitation. Gracián finds that the Spanish personality, choleric and serious, is gifted with a spirited imagination.[3] Imagination, according to Gracián, demands maturity and depends on age: the span of a vigorous imagination lasts thirty to forty years, with its keenest activity during middle age. This belief complements the metaphoric division of man's life into *primavera* ("spring"), *otoño* ("fall"), and *invierno* ("winter") found in *The Master Critic*.

Since imagination, a facet of ingenio, makes possible the poet's skill in associating ideas and images, Gracián concludes that it complements the intellect, where the latter is conceived of as knowledge. Ingenio as imagination, therefore, is a productive faculty in that it is an aid to the intellect in attaining truth and in being disposed to accept *what is not* in the poem.[4]

As for invention, Gracián states that this is a very arduous and almost impossible task: "Allá en la Edad de Oro se inventaban . . .; ya todo es repetir ("Back in the Golden Age, they invented . . .; now everything is repetition").[5] Nevertheless, Gracián considers invention to be a faculty synonymous with both agudeza and imagination in the creation of poetry through new combinations of the literary experience (see preceding chapter, pp. 31ff.).[6] The poet must create from his own personal fund of imagery, thought, feeling, and intellectual culture, but he must make use only of difficult and worthwhile subjects:

The matter is the foundation for invention; it gives footing to the subtlety. There is "objective wit" already in the objects themselves, such as enigmas, quandaries, and *crisis*, if one works with them; then the imagination arrives and elevates the search. Some writers are as abundant as others are sterile, but there is none so empty that a good mind cannot find something to take as prey, by conformity or contrast, singling it out by means of confrontation. (p. 898; 513a)

Although his aesthetics emphasizes the creative act, Gracián also recognizes the poet's need to imitate and learn from the ancient masters. Following the seventeenth-century Aristotelian theory of imitation[7] as imitation of great poets, Gracián strongly praises the poets of Latin antiquity and the Italian Renaissance. However, his interpretation of imitation consists *not* in copying the work but rather in the transfiguration of its ideas. The poet is to find inspiration in previous artistic expression, to recreate the work without acknowledging its origin and to borrow and adapt a work as he wishes.

In short, Gracián develops a unique concept of poetry in his belief that la verdad poética stresses the function of poetry as one of revealing a poetic, imaginative truth,[8] along with providing pleasure. Imagination is the power to associate ideas and images, whereas invention is the potential of the individual to write creatively. In more specific terms, Gracián views poetry in various ways, thereby following his own classical precept of *la hermosa variedad* ("attractive variety"). His concept of poetry, stressing the profundity of the idea, lies within the framework of the aesthetic that poetry is (1) intellectual play, (2) drama, (3) myth, (4) humor, and (5) commitment. Therefore, *The Mind's Wit* focuses on a multiplicity of issues concerning poetry;[9] the following analysis will treat each in turn.

1. Poetry as Intellectual Play

In the aesthetics of Gracián, poetry is *belleza* ("beauty"), and the most dynamic aspect of beauty lies within the realm of intellectual and abstract ideas which are created by agudeza, ingenio, and concepto. Mental ingenuity, clever technical effects, intricate structure, and wordplay are the poet's ingredients for the creation of a serious poetry which challenges and plays with the intellect. The *Agudeza* makes reference to many examples of this type of difficult and intellectual poetry. Those poets, however, who are the most ingenious and brilliant of all are Martial and Góngora.

The Roman poet Martial represents the apex of intellectual poetry; he is "el primogénito de la agudeza" ("the primogenitor of wit"). His epigram-sonnets (there is no distinction between the two forms in Gracián's terminology) reveal great ideas, sensitive sentiments, and a skilled craftsmanship in the use of allusions, illogical conclusions, parallels, antitheses, similes, maxims, puns, and other devices. The keenness of his mind is exemplified in the capacity to think in universal terms and in his poetic treatment of many themes. For example, his poems of a pure, intellectual nature mentioned by Gracián include: Rome's fires for Germanicus ("Quantas, Io, latias mundi conventus ad aras"), the plight of a melancholy and rich man ("Quum cathedralicos portet tibi rehda ministros"), Caesar's greatness ("Inter Caesareae discrimina saeva Dianae"), praise and criticism of Fabula ("Omnes aut vetulas habes amicas").

Likewise, the poetic creation of Luis de Góngora, "el culto poeta, cisne en los conceptos, águila en los conceptos" ("the learned poet, swan in conceits, eagle in conceits"), is another intellectual monument. *The Mind's Wit* downplays the *culteranista* poetry of Góngora's *Polifemo* (Polyphemus) and the *Soledades* (Solitudes), usually recognized now as Góngora's major works, in order to demonstrate and praise the technical artistry and brilliant ideas found in Góngora's more popular poetry, such as the ballads, sonnets, and canciones, and in the comdy *Las firmezas de Isabela* (The Constancy of Isabela). Gracián stresses those poems by Góngora which have conceptual contents and which also reveal a notable command of poetic devices, such as wordplay, concealed explanations, hyperbole, metaphor, erudite and hermetic allusions, epithets, and subtle allusions. Góngora's thought-provoking and delightful themes include, for instance, the essence of time, the brevity of life, a comparison of Christ's birth with his death, the condemnation of jealousy to hell, a panegyric for the historian Luis de Babia, and a panegyric for Henry IV of Spain.

2. Poetry as Drama

Other examples from the poetry in *The Mind's Wit* reflect Gracián's awareness of the dramatic nature of poetry. By this Gracián means that the poet is writing for a reader with whom he is emotionally involved. The elements of dialogue, exclamation, hyperbole, and interrogation are prominent in the work, and emotional intensity highlights the intellectual acuteness of the poem. One observes that Gracián prefers a subjective and personal type of poetry in his aesthetics. Two of the many artists mentioned in the *The Mind's Wit* who particularly represent the dramatic quality of poetry are the Portuguese Camões and Lope de Vega.

Camões is the poet of love, "that celebrated poet" who is "grave, sútil y conceptuoso" ("grave, subtle and conceitful"). His poems (Gracián gives the titles in Spanish) "¿Como ficeste Porcia tal ferida?" (Portia, how did you wound so?), "Mi corazón me han robado" (They have stolen my heart), and "Apartábase Nise de Montano" (Nise left Montano) are a few examples of the tendency to dramatize and heighten the emotional experience of human love by means of dialogue, questioning, and searching.

Emotion and drama are carried to even greater lengths in religious poetry. Gracián, as a Jesuit, is particularly sensitive to the divine and sacred thoughts in his numerous quotations of poetry. The poet addresses himself to the Supreme Being or to the saints with feelings of emotion which increase tension and subtlety. Lope de Vega, "el fecundo y copioso poeta" ("that fertile and copious poet"), is valued for his dramatic poetry portraying the human situation of man as both sinner and saint. "Oh engaño de los hombres, vida breve" (Oh betrayer of men, short life), "Canción al Santísimo" (Song to the Sacred Sacrament), and "Peregrino Abraham, intenta asilo" (Pilgrim Abraham, seek asylum)—all intensify the emotional interaction with divine love, and so influence the reader emotionally as well as intellectually.

3. Poetry as Myth

The concept of erudition is reiterated throughout *The Mind's Wit*. Knowledge and understanding are true manifestations of the literary virtues of agudeza and ingenio. The gifted and versatile poet, therefore, knows all arts and sciences, including the Greco-Roman myths. In this way, Gracián conceives of the poem as mythic embodiment: poetry has contact and identification with myths. The presence of myths within the poem delights and engages the mind on the basis of their difficulty and obscurity, thereby forming an attractive and original conceit. A few poets whose compositions embody myths are Tito Vespasiano Strozzi, Quevedo, Lope de Vega, Lupercio Leonardo de Argensola, Bartolomé Leonardo de Argensola, and Juan de Arguijo.

4. Poetry as Humor

Burlesque, satiric, and comic poetry is approved by Gracián, who follows another Horatian principle, that of "ridentem dicere verum" ("to tell the truth with a laugh"). Therefore, the light mood of the spontaneous and jocular poetic examples in *The Mind's Wit* contrasts with sublime and serious poetry. Our critic highly praises the intellectual liveliness of humorous poetry, which is less artistic but far more popular for its capacity to entertain and to amuse. Gracián values all types of humor, whether it be the practical humor of Martial, the earthy comedy of Baltasar de Alcázar, the comical exaggeration of Góngora, or the misanthropic satire of Quevedo. Humor, therefore, is for Gracián an application of the broad Horatian *dulce et utile* doctrine. Furthermore, it is strongly linked with ingenio, allowing the poet to remain several jumps ahead of his reader.

5. Poetry as Commitment

Our Aragonese critic affirms a correlation between poetic expression and the tendency to moralize. His view that the poet is the conveyor of old truths and the discoverer of new ones points to a rather modern frame of reference in that poetry is to be committed to the human condition. He supports the age-old idea that the poet does not write for himself but for others and that the voice of the people influences the fate of an artistic work. Therefore, the content of the poem not only attracts the intellect, engenders sentiment, and entertains, but poetry also teaches as it interprets the human situation. *The Mind's Wit* records many didactic poems which again reveal Gracián's commitment to life. Examples discussed of poems of this nature concern the capriciousness of time, the effects of profane love, the suffering found in solitude, disillusionment, and memory in the sonnets of Garcilaso de la Vega and Antonio de Mendoza, Francisco de Borja y Aragón, el Príncipe de Esquilache, "Príncipe de la Poesía" ("Prince of Poetry"), also dedicates an eclogue to solitude and the isolation of man. The human condition is reflected also in Gracián's selection of poems dealing with woman. Luis de Carrillo y Sotomayor dwells on woman's deceits in a sonnet, and Lope de Vega writes on the satanic yet beautiful creative nature of women as it is epitomized in the Blessed Virgin, and, in spite of his supposed misogyny, Gracián reveals an attitude of appreciation for women. One of the many poets cited in this respect is Marino, who wrote sonnets to the Blessed Virgin.

The brief foregoing analysis gives a schematic idea of Gracián's approach to various functions and characteristics of poetry. Since he does not examine poetry in all its aspects but only in its intrinsic relationship to wit, it has been necessary to draw inferences based on his recurring patterns of thought on the subject. Certainly as a critic Gracián is well aware of the major literatures of the Western tradition and recognizes the aspects of agudeza and concepto in all genres and literary works; they are especially present in poetry. Thus, Gracián's concept of the poem takes into account many facets: poetry appears as truth, beauty, imagination, creation, imitation, intellectual play, drama, myth, humor, and commitment. Gracián, sensitive to poetry as the "art of arts," knows that poetry extends to all levels of human experience and appreciates it as the culmination of literary expression in its inclusion of every type of agudeza.

II   *Aspects of Literary Composition*

The Mind's Wit goes beyond a simple cataloguing of the types of wit and their manifestations in literary works. Gracián succeeds in defining the literary act of creation in broad terms through his evaluation of several aspects of literary composition: (1) style, (2) erudition, (3) good taste, and (4) the ineffable.

1. Style

In Part II, Discourses 60, 61, and 62 explore the stylistic systems available to writers. Gracián's principal tenet, "Lo bueno, si breve, dos veces bueno" ("if that which is good is short, it's twice as good"), summarizes his preferred formula that echoes Horace's "brevis esse laboro" ("I strive to be concise"). The theory of brevity is reinforced by his theory of rapidity: not only is this witticism quick in time, but it is so in words; fast and neat: two lustres [i.e., brilliances] (p. 619; 414b). The laconic style which Gracián recommends—for him it is characteristically *el estilo natural* ("natural style")—recalls conceptism and its goal of expressing truth succinctly and compactly. It is Gracián's opinion that Mateo Alemán is the most skillful writer of this style.

Gracián subordinates culteranism to conceptism when he speaks of the artistic and complicated *culto,* or *Attic,* style. He disagrees with the idea of art for art's sake, although he esteems highly the flowery language of Góngora, many of whose followers he nevertheless condemns. Their writings are "hojas de palabras" ("sheets of words") that lack agudeza and ideas. In passing, it is interesting to observe that Gracián expresses an idea later to be reformulated by the twentieth-century critic, Dámaso Alonso, when he says that Góngora was not the first to write in the culto style, but that he merely intensified and brought to its culmination a style which has its antecedents in a long rhetorical tradition:

> But let us come now to the mannered style, which displays more on this idea of ingeniousness than that of pure judgment, which attends rather to the outstanding phrase than to the flowery manner. The Phoenix of this style, not so much because he was first, for Apuleius in Latin and don Luis

Carrillo in Spanish had already practiced it, but because he made it soar to its highest point, was don Luis de Góngora, especially in his *Polifemo* [Polyphemus] and his *Soledades* [Solitudes]. There have been some who wanted to follow him, like Icarus after Daedalus; they pick phrases (like the man who imitated the King of Naples' quirk of twisting his mouth), and inculcate them into their work, so that their whole culture may be reduced to four or six little words. (pp. 890—91; 510b)

Other of Gracián's ideas on style included a disdain for clumsy versification as well as the excessive dependence on adjectives and epithets. The nexus of style is in the verb, which perfects expression by its power to suggest, emphasize, and indicate ideas. Gracián's final consideration of style rests on a moderate position that corresponds to his eclectic and comprehensive view of what literature is and should be. He prescribes the "medium style," which finds a balance of what he calls the natural and adorned styles.

Furthermore, our critic makes a very contemporary value judgment in that he considers the totality of style as the result of the structural integration of the work. A poem, for example, is composed of words which are to convey meaning; however, it is only when the complex structure as meaning expresses a unity that totality in the work is achieved. Gracián sees that unity between content (emphasized in the *conceptista* approach) and form (emphasized in the *culteranista* expression) exists in imaginative writing. Unity and concision contribute to the perfection of art; the baroque goal of absolute unity dominates the aesthetics of the Jesuit, who sees that content and form are tightly interwoven. Therefore, to communicate the whole of the literary experience is difficult and arduous, but it is the writer's ultimate goal:

A whole, in physical composition as well as in artificial, is always the most noble, the ultimate object, and the adequate end of the arts; and though its perfection results from that of its parts, it adds the greater one of graceful union. It is an arduous business, but difficulty was never a discredit, nor is simplicity always an advantage. What is worthwhile is costly, and vice versa. (p. 762; 459b)

2. Erudition

The concept of erudition is consistently discussed in Renaissance and baroque poetics: for example, the *Cisne de Apolo* (Apollo's Swan 1602) by Luis A. de Carballo, the *Libro de la erudición poética* (Book of Poetic Erudition 1611) by Luis Carillo y Sotomayor. These writings, *The Mind's Wit* included, require the poet-writer to be well versed in all areas of knowledge. It must be remembered that the idea of erudition underlies all of Gracián's works, especially *The Master Critic*.[12] However, in *The Mind's Wit*, erudition is a major principle which applies to the reader as well as to the author. Gracián's consideration of erudition reflects several major ideas of *The Mind's Wit*. He is constant in his praise for the educated man and in his scorn for the *vulgo*, "the masses."

Some of the sources of erudition, the Jesuit claims, are to be found in sacred or human history, philosophy, maxims, emblems, parables, and allegories. He cites erudition as the crowning touch of any piece of literature and maintains that any literary work of value reveals erudite substance: "Without erudition, neither sermons nor conversation nor books have either pleasure or substance about them (pp. 838—39; 489a). Even imagination has recourse to erudition in order to find correspondences which exist in life.[13]

The concept of erudition also brings to mind the age-old quarrel of the ancients versus the moderns.[14] Gracián's attitude toward the issue is ambivalent. Earlier in the treatise, he enthusiastically defends the erudition of the ancient writers, whose writings reflect the soul of agudeza. Later, the moderns rank in superiority, for their works are more intellectually challenging, original, and less overrated by the critics:

> Erudition in modern things is often even more flavorful than that in antiquity, and more often listened to, though less exalted. The sayings and deeds of the ancients are rather well picked over; modern examples, if sublime, delight with their novelty, and enlightenment may be doubled by their unusualness and ingenious accommodation. (p. 840; 489b)

Erudition, in sum, is an integral part of the creation of conceits in the literary work. It is associated with the intellect and the imagination, and its function is practical as well as aesthetic.

3. *Buen gusto*

Gracián's theorizing about literature includes an orientation for *buen gusto* ("good taste"). Critics have recognized Gracián as one of the first formulators of the term, which is extensively used in all of his works.[15] In 1894 Karl Borinski named him "El Padre de Buen Gusto" ("the Father of Good Taste").[16] The description that Maldonado de Guevara gives of Gracián's concept of buen gusto is most pertinent, for he finds that the Jesuit is a precursor of Kant's idea of aesthetic taste:

> For Kant good taste (that is, decorum) is above all a judging, a pure judgment. And this same characteristic is found in Gracián. It is not a matter of spontaneous and mysterious intuition, but of a judgment of values based on the non-conceptual feeling of that which is beautiful. It is a matter of judgment which is not based on the concepts and judgments, determinants proper to Logic and Science, because it is above all, a reflective that moves among aesthetic values.[17]

Gracián's buen gusto is thus the exercise of intuitional and subjective reasoning.

In *The Mind's Wit*, buen gusto is equated with decorum in that Gracián's conception of beauty lies within order, fitness and good taste. He always speaks of the appropriate uses of the literary work:

> Some authorities are sacred and should be adjusted [i.e., accommodated] to serious things, to decent things. . . . On the other hand, when a text from secular learning is adjusted to holy matters, it must be sublime and on a worthwhile subject. (pp. 577–78; 402b–403a)

> . . . even adages and proverbs avail a great deal, but they must generally be selected in order to avoid vulgarity. (p. 841; 490b)

Decorum, buen gusto, regulates content and form in that epithets must use an appropriate adjectivization and the *romance* ("ballad") form requires bold rather than profound conceits. The *quintilla* ("a five-verse strophe") should be written with better than average conceits. Gracián suggests that the writer employ practical sense in order to fit subject matter to form, and his theory of buen gusto may be briefly summarized as a very rational and subjective activity.

4. *No sé qué*

That Gracián is the great critical voice of the Spanish seventeenth century is particularly evident in his treatment of the *no sé qué* ("the ineffable"), although this critical term is more implied than described in *The Mind's Wit*.[18] Porqueras-Mayo contends that Gracián is a possible precursor of Feijoo's theory of the no sé qué in the eighteenth century.[19] However, in *The Mind's Wit*, there are many allusions to no sé qué in the sense that the invention of plots does not depend on precepts but rather on the moment and circumstances of creation. Speaking of the resourcefulness of the imagination, Gracián states its quality of no sé qué:

O, how resourceful the mind in unforeseen events! By reason of what is set before it, it grows under pressure until it hardly recognizes itself. In the other species of wit the mind reasons; in this one [i.e., "on Wit Through Acquiring Oneself in Deed"] it flies, and, just as a triumphant plant, not only does not yield to weight nor surrender to suffocation, but when pressed expands and begins to loom up until crowned with the rays of the sun. (p. 698; 437b)

The art of Lope de Vega with its witty and subtle expression is an act of the spirit—that inexplicable facet of the creative act: "A witticism difficult because of its sublime matter and subtle because of its enhancement from skill is an act worthy and proper of the spirit; . . ." (p. 102; 241b).

Indeed certain and infallible rules for regulating writing are impossible in the sense that a prominent position must always be given uncircumscribed creativity. The mind's genius which exists beyond the realm of the rules of rhetoric, gives birth to creation: "Certain and infallible rules for regulating these subtle inferences cannot be given. The mind's boldness and vigor alone suffice for so extravagant a discourse" (p. 629; 417b).

The indescribable and the inexpressible in literary creation, the *je ne sais quoi* of seventeenth-century French literature and the no sé qué of Feijoo in eighteenth-century Spanish literature, are terms which derive ultimately from Cicero, but which, as Porqueras-Mayo shows, represent a typical aspect of Gracián's views, for Gracián is one of the first critics to study the concept to any extent in Romance literature.

III *Literary Preferences of* The Mind's Wit[20]

An examination of Gracián's theories on poetry naturally includes his literary preferences—the works to which he refers as illustrations of his literary ideas. *The Mind's Wit,* if seen in one of its most important lights—that of a prose work of eulogistic criticism—may be compared with those previous laudatory poems *El Canto de Calíope* (Caliope's Song) by Cervantes and *El Laurel de Apolo* (Apollo's Laurel) and *Las Epístolas* (Epistles) by Lope de Vega.[21] However, the contribution of the Jesuit critic is superior because of the scope of his critical opinions, which consider literature of all genres and forms in universal, national, and regional terms.

Two dominant factors figure in the formulation of Gracián's literary preferences. One is that he is a Jesuit, and therefore he is especially well versed in the literary tradition of Classical Latin. He was, as already seen, very knowledgeable in the postclassical literatures that preceded his own time. His literary experience, therefore, involved a compendium of much of the literature written previous to his own era.

Curtius has suggested a parallel between Gracián and the writers of the Latin Silver Age in that Gracián prefers the authors of that age who are manneristic, that is, intellectual writers like himself: Martial, Seneca, Pliny the Younger, Tacitus, Florus, Velleuis Paterculus, Valerius Maximus, Lucan, Frontinus, Persius, Apuleius, Ausonius, Claudian, and Pendatius.[22] But after Martial it is Horace who is quoted most often.[23] Gracián praises the *Metamorphoses* of Ovid and the *Aeneid* of Virgil on the basis of their inventive and complicated narratives as well as for their erudition.

The Patristic literary tradition is well represented in *The Mind's Wit:* Clement of Alexandria, Origen, St. Gregory Nazianzus, and St. John the Damascene. Gracián is particularly devoted to the sermons of St. Augustine, St. Ambrose, and St. Peter Chrysologus, who all represent the *anómalo* ("anomalous") method of literary expression. The latter is an inventive, spontaneous expression, as opposed to the dry and dull, *adjustado* ("tight, confined") method of Origen and his followers. Although medieval writers are virtually ignored, Gracián mentions St. Bernard of Clairvaux and St. Thomas Aquinas, and he quotes an epigram of Matthew of Vendôme, although without giving him credit.[24] Gracián's defense of the theological works of St. Thomas Aquinas comes later in *The Master Critic.*

Latin writers of the Renaissance are frequently mentioned in *The Mind's Wit* as practitioners of agudeza, ingenio, and concepto: "El

culto" ("the learned") Giovanni Pontano, Italian poet and
historian, and the Italian poets Gerolamo Angeriano, Tito Vesasiano
Strozzi, Andrelinus, and Julius Caesar Scaliger. Joseph Justo
Scaliger is cited once for a translation into Latin of a Greek poem.
Leo X is quoted for his ingenious prose, while Urban VIII merits
mention for his poetry and witty use of language. However, it is
Alciato who wins most extensive praise and citation for his
Emblemata (Book of Emblems). The emblems complement
Gracián's theory of brevity and difficulty, and the intellectual
conceit and visual appeal of the emblem are other reasons why the
form is a favorite of Gracián in *The Mind's Wit*.[25] Two Frenchmen
are included in this tradition: the humorist Marc Antoine Muret
and the Jesuit poet François Remond. Jaime Juan Falcón, "El
Martial de Valencia" (Valencia's Martial), Juan Lorenzo Palmireno,
"el aragonés Horacio" (the Aragonese Horace), also figure in this
Renaissance Latin tradition.

The nonfictional writings of history and politics enter into
Gracián's literary considerations. It is his opinion that history and
politics are a means for the writer to interpret and comment upon
life and its events. A few historians are casually mentioned from the
sixteenth century: Antonio de Fuenmayor, also cited in *The Master
Critic*, is praised for his remarkable "medium style" in his *Vida de
San Pío V* (The Life of St. Pius V). Seventeenth-century writers
include Pierre Matthieu, who is designated as "el insigne
historiador de Francia" ("the outstanding historian of France"),
Luis Cabrera de Córdoba, whose style is "affected," Luis de Bavia,
who is praised for his "terse and elegant" style. The latter is
esteemed for his translation of the work of Gracián's favorite Italian
historian, Girolamo de Franchi Constaggio, the *Unión del Reino del
Portugal con Castilla* (The Union of the Kingdoms of Portugal and
Castile). Another Italian, Virgilio Malvezzi, interprets history by
combining a perfect sententious style with critical insights. And of
all the seventeenth-century Spanish historians, the Augustinian,
Padre Juan Márquez, "el benemérito de la lengua española"
("worthy of the Spanish language"), is cited for his profound and
prudent style, comparable to the style of Tacitus. Gracián quotes
from chapter 38 of *El gobierno cristiano* (Christian Government).

Three Italian writers fit within the framework of Gracián's
general theory that literature reflects life. *El galateo cortesano*

(Galateo) by Giovanni della Casa, a handbook of manners from the sixteenth century, is eulogized for its influence upon all nations, Spain included; it even inspired our critic's own famous work, *The Discreet Man*. Traiano Boccalini, "que supo juntar lo precioso con lo ingenioso" ("who knew how to join the precious with the ingenious"), is another favorite satirical and critical writer of the seventeenth century whom Gracián highly esteems and frequently quotes. *I ragguali di Parnaso* (Reports from Parnassus) furnishes Gracián with much interesting material to quote. The significant political writer, also of the seventeenth century, Giovanni Botero, ranks for Gracián among the best modern writers for his wit and his political anecdotes. Among Botero's works, Gracián praises *Della ragione di stato* (Concerning Raison d'Etat, 1589) and *Delle relazioni universali* (Concerning Universal Relations). It is interesting to note that both Boccalini and Botero continue in high favor a few years later in *The Master Critic*.

The Mind's Wit is filled with quotations from sermons: cited are almost 130 sermons by Jesuits, friends of Gracián, and members of other orders. The importance of the sermon lies in its intellectual ideas and didactic intent. Therefore, Gracián considers it a brilliant literary form. This idea, of course, complements the seventeenth-century Spanish opinion that the sermon has aesthetic value, as seen in the quantity of treatises on preaching, which far exceed in number those dealing with literary theory.[26] Among the most prominent sermonists are Hernando de Santiago, "el mayor orador de su siglo" ("the greatest orator of his century"), Francisco Suárez, author of *Contra Regem Angliae*, "el erudito y conceptuso" ("the learned and conceitful") Pedro de Valderrama, Padre Jerónimo de Florencia, "el Ambrosio de este siglo" ("this century's Ambrose"), the Portuguese fathers, Francisco de Mendoza, who excels in sermon writing *(Viridarium* and *Sermones del tiempo* [Sermons on Time]), and Diogo Lopes de Andrade. Gracián frequently praises the theologian and humanist Hortensio Félix Paravicino, and his own brother, Felipe Gracián, for their eloquence and brilliance.

In addition to the sermon, the apothegm or maxim ranks as another notable literary form. Its brevity, spontaneous wit, and didacticism attract Gracián, who takes his examples from such writers of classical antiquity as Plutarch, Diogenes Laertius,

Valerius Maximus, and Suetonius. The modern writers also communicate by means of the favored form. Gracián draws heavily from the *Floresta española* (Spanish Anthology) of Melchor de Santa Cruz. Likewise, Juan Rufo, the "ingenioso Jurado de Córdoba" ("the ingenious Cordoban Juror"), cited thirty-seven times in *The Mind's Wit*, is praised for his poetry but more so for his *Seiscientos apoftegmas* [sic] (600 Maxims), which is "uno de los libros del buen gusto" ("one of the books in good taste").

Prose fiction is not slighted in the aesthetics of Gracián. To a modern's surprise, Cervantes gets no mention (but then, few of his contemporaries recognized his importance, although one could well wish Gracián, of all of them, had been the exception). The Jesuit recognizes the value of some prose fiction. He loves the ingenuity and the didactic intent found in Heliodorus's early Greek novel, *Theogenes and Chariclea*. Apuleius's *Golden Ass* is also rated as great allegorical fiction, and Gracián admits that he finds the story of Cupid and Psyche particularly entertaining on the basis of its moral intent. Likewise, John Barclay's novel *Argenis* is mentioned as having been influenced by Heliodorus. The two giants of prose fiction, however, are don Juan Manuel, author of *El Conde Lucanor* (Tales of Count Lucanor), and Mateo Alemán, author of *Guzmán de Alfarache*. These frequently quoted writers represent the apex of successful writing and for Gracián theirs was a delightful type of artistry which entertains and instructs, and a meaningful truth is attained through the perfect combination of *prodesse et delectare*.

As Sánchez Escribano[27] has pointed out, the theater is given less attention in *The Mind's Wit* than any other literary form. Nevertheless, some interesting and original observations are made by our critic. For instance, Gracián renders a very personal opinion when he mentions that the "ingenious" *Tragicomedia de Calixto y Melibea* (Tragicomedy of Calixto and Melibea) was written by "un cubierto aragonés" ("an Aragonese in disguise"). Gracián views the contemporary theater with cautious reservation. He ranks the Spanish national theater below the drama of that superior playwright Guarini, "el Fénix de Italia" ("Italy's Phoenix"), and the author of the famous *Pastor Fido*. What is most significant, however, is the Jesuit's thumbnail sketch of the history of the theater in Discourse 45. The pastoral drama of the "prodigious" Lope de Rueda receives enthusiastic endorsement, as do the *capa y espada* plays, *La dama duende* (The Phantom Lady) and *La casa con dos puertas* (A House with Two Doors), both by Calderón de la Barca. And although Gracián disdains the careless and copious style of Lope de Vega, an artist of the popular masses, the Jesuit appreciates the *agudeza* of his art of comedy and justifies it on the basis of its moral message. The comedies mentioned include *El villano en su rincón* (The Farmer's Home is His Castle), *Con su pan se lo coma*) Take the Bitter with the Sweet), *La dama boba* (The Scatterbrain), *Los melindres de Belisa* (Belisa's Pruderies), and *El dómine Lucas* (Master Lucas). The drama clearly is not a literary preference of the Aragonese critic, but the dramatic intrigues attract him. As J. M. Cossío observes, Gracián's approach to the contemporary theater of Spain is distinctly independent and audacious to the extent that he ignores most of the major dramatists, choosing instead to praise minor ones like Antonio Hurtado de Mendoza and Jerónimo de Villayzán.[28] It is also curious to note that no reference is made in *The Mind's Wit* to Agustín Moreto, the only dramatist mentioned in *The Master Critic*.

The Mind's Wit is most informative in its discussions of poetry, for Gracián the most sublime of literary genres. As in *The Master Critic*, much literature is seen in national terms, and this national consciousness is most obvious in Gracián's treatment of poetry.

The Italian poets are not neglected. Dante is merely praised for the allegorical poetry of the *Inferno*, while Petrarch receives more attention. Gracián approves of the latter's *Triumphs*, but condemns his displeasing and sensual love sonnets, as he is to do again in *The Master Critic*. Tasso, mentioned in the prologue as "el valiente" ("the valiant one"), is cited only once. Gracián, however, is extravagant in his eulogy of Giambattista Marino and Giambattista Guarini, two notable poets of the seventeenth century whose sacred and profane poetry in the *conceptista* manner supports Gracián's literary doctrine. The latter describes Marino as "el delicado" ("the delicate one"), "el culto" ("the learned one"), or "el conceptuoso" ("the conceitful one"), while Guarini is mostly identified as "el caballero" ("the gentleman").

Gracián's appraisal of Portuguese poetry is limited to four poets from the sixteenth century. Diogo [sic] de Brandão and Francisco Sá de Miranda are cursorily mentioned, and near the end of the treatise, Gracián expresses a regret for not having quoted from the poetry of the former. It is the "celebrated" Camões who is the perfect poet of love. Gracián praises him effusively, quotes him frequently, and appreciates his sonnets written in both Portuguese and Spanish, as well as his *Lusiads.* Gracián also esteems Jorge de Montemayor for his rare and affected poetic language in *Los siete libros de Diana* (Diana's Seven Books).

To some extent, *The Mind's Wit* may be considered a small anthology of Spanish poetry, for Gracián comments extensively on the "ancients"—the Spanish medieval poets—and upon the "modern" poets who wrote during the Golden Age of Spain. Again, the critic's insights are very perceptive, and his judgments continue to have value for us today. Discourses 24 and 25 discuss several medieval poets, whose poems are quoted from the *Cancionero general de Hernando del Castillo* (Hernando del Castillo's General Songbook). Lope de Sosa, Garci Sánchez de Badajoz, Carlos de Guevara, Diego de San Pedro, Juan de Tapia—all are praised for their clever and subtle poetry. And Gracián quotes a series of Juan de Mena's "conceptos enigmáticos" ("enigmatic conceits"); although the reader recognizes them as Mena's, Gracián curiously fails to give Mena direct credit for them.

Gracián's interpretation of sixteenth-century Spanish poetry reveals understandably personal biases. Garcilaso, like Camões, is a perfect poet in both subject matter and technique. Gracián quotes ten of his sonnets and commends him without reservation as "el dulce" ("the sweet one"), "el propio y el atento" ("the proper and attentive one"), or "el más canoro cisne del Tajo" ("the Tajo's most melodious swan"). Fray Luis de León, on the other hand, is quoted infrequently. It is curious that the Aragonese critic is not drawn to the intellectual and somber poetry of that most "learned and grave" of poets. Other judgments of sixteenth-century poets include negative opinions concerning the sensual poetry of Fernando de Herrera and high praise for the great wits, Baltasar de Alcázar, Gregorio Silvestre, and Francisco de Figueroa.

Concerning the poetry of the seventeenth century, Correa Calderón offers a noteworthy observation in his belief that *The Mind's Wit,* although stressing conceptism, records more cultista poetry.[29] The independent Jesuit approves of all poetic movements of his country, however, and among the *culteranos* he particularly favors Góngora and Luis Carrillo y Sotomayor. However, Gracián does not favor the Góngora of the famous *Polifemo* and *Soledades*. On the contrary, he praises and quotes the sonnets and *letrillas* ("rondelets") as well as the ballads of the "most acute and ingenious" Góngora, who uses irony, word play, satire and humor. Next to martial, Góngora is cited more that any other poet in *The Mind's Wit*, where he is acclaimed the "monstruo en todo" ("monster [prodigy] in everything"). Many cultista sonnets of Luis Carrillo de Sotomayor are praised, but Gracián frequently suggests that Carrillo's art is limited by its lack of moralizing. Other *culteranistas* who receive enthusiastic mention in the treatise include Francisco López de Zárate, Gabriel de Bocángel, Anastasio Pantaleón de Ribera, and Hortensio Félix Paravicino. Adolph Coster notes that Góngora and Paravicino are always referred to as *bizarros* ("bizarre") or *cultos poetas* ("learned poets"), while Lope and Quevedo are the *conceptuoso* ("conceitful"), or *ingenioso* ("ingenious") artists.[30] Quevedo ranks as the champion of conceptista poetry in *The Mind's Wit*. Gracián appreciates his intellectual poems, and quotes a number of sonnets and madrigals which reveal the poet's artistic imagination, versatility, and wit. Alonso de Ledesma, "the divine poet," and the Conde de Villamediana, who is credited with amalgamating the sententious and the critical, follow the conceptista current; their poems are frequently quoted.

Among the poets of the seventeenth century, Gracián recognizes a group of independent and eclectic artists. Lope, "la más fértil vega" ("that most fertile meadow [a play on his surname Vega, "meadow"]"), "más conceptuoso que bizarro" ("more conceitful than bizarre [marvelous]"), heads the group. The "monstruo de la naturaleza" ("monster of nature") is quoted some thirty-five times. Gracián admires his sacred and profane poetry as well as his versatility. What bothers our critic is that Lope's literature is popular rather than aristocratic in nature. Juan de Arguijo, Antonio Hurtado de Mendoza, and Juan Pérez de Montalbán also figure in this group of independent and ingenious poets. And it is interesting to note that Salas Barbadillo and Vélez de Guevara, two famous picaresque novelists, appear in *The Mind's Wit* as poets. Salas Barbadillo is erudite and witty, while Vélez de Guevara is commended for his clever poetic technique of accumulating synonyms.

The Aragonese *literati* deserve special attention in this survey, for Gracián draws from a wealth of writers, friends, and family from his native Aragón. To some extent, Gracián departs from analytical and objective evaluation and becomes quite personal when he evaluates literature in regional terms. Although his evaluation is subjective, he contributes an important bibliographic catalogue of Aragonese literature, along with many insights into the letters of the region. Gracián takes great pride in quoting extensively from Martial, stressing his Aragonese background and endorsing him as the most intellectual and witty of poets. Gracián's friend Manuel de Salinas is cited seventy-six times in the treatise, mostly for his brilliant translations of Martial's poetry. Two other favorites are the Argensola brothers; the Jesuit admires the subtlety of their thought as well as their technical skill in writing *tercetos* ("tercets"), a judgment which he repeats in *The Master Critic*. Our critic, however, subordinates the art of Lupercio to that of Bartolomé: the latter is far more talented in that he is the philosopher-poet. Nevertheless, Gracián is constant in his effusive praise for the two brothers, who are "el non plus ultra del Parnaso" ("the *non plus ultra* of Parnassus"). A striking and unique aspect of Gracián's literary criticism is his concern for women poets, one excellent reason for not dismissing him as a misogynist; he also refers to several female historical figures. Aragonese poetesses, true artists of agudeza and ingenio, include Ana Francisca Abarca de Bolea, Doña Hipólita de Narváez, María Nieto de Aragón, Madre Madalena de la Presentación, Ana Vicencia de Mendoza, and Doña Luciana de Narváez. The poetic contributions include both religious and secular poetry.

Gracián draws from a host of other writers also. He mentions the poetry of his brother Fray Pedro Gracián, Pedro Liñán de Riaza, Juan Lorenzo Ibáñez, "cisne del Ebro" ("the swan of the Ebro"), the sermons of his brothers Felipe and Fray Reimundo, his cousin Fray Reimundo, and Juan Palafox y Mendoza, the writings of the historian Juan Francisco Andrés de Uztarroz, the erudite works of Josep Pellicer.

In summary, if one were to synthesize briefly the literary preferences of Gracián in *The Mind's Wit*, the result would be a profile of the witty and sententious poet Martial, the moral literature of don Juan Manuel, Mateo Alemán, the emblematic literature of Alciato, the sensitive and well-written poetry of Camões, the sweet poetry of Góngora, the versatility of Lope, the humor and satiric wit of Quevedo, the sophisticated and difficult poetry of Marino and Guarini, the philosophic and technical excellence of the Argensola brothers, and the brilliant sermons of his brother Felipe Gracián.

IV   The Mind's Wit *and the Baroque*

No study of Gracián's literary ideas would be complete without a summary of the ways in which he elucidates baroque aesthetics. Twentieth-century scholars have taken a vital interest in the evaluation of the ambiguous term "baroque,"[31] a word which covers a wide range of norms, literary techniques, and precepts. Yet for an interpretation of the baroque literary age one need only turn to the famous *Mind's Wit*, which is a brilliant manifesto of baroque literary theory. The Jesuit critic defined the what and why of Spanish as well as European literary creation and was the first Spaniard to identify and to stress several aspects of seventeenth-century literature which present-day critics term the baroque. *The Mind's Wit* quotes over a thousand examples of prose and poetry written in the classical and Western traditions; some five hundred of these are from writers of Spain's Golden Age.

Baroque literature is distinctive because it is principally although perhaps not exclusively (e.g., Lope's comedy) a literature for an aristocratic and cultured audience. The importance of the reader to the author was most evident in the flourishing existence of the prologue during the Golden Age. In the seventeenth-century prologue, or *a quien leyere* ("to whoever may read this"), the author reveals a concern for establishing rapport with the reader, and the literary work depends on the interaction of the author and his public.

The Mind's Wit and Gracián's other works show that for him the reader is properly limited to the cultured and erudite few of society. The masses are utterly disdained, while the élite reading public is considered the final judge of literature; this assumes the capacity of the reader to rise to the challenge offered by the conceptista literature that Gracián loved. In *The Mind's Wit*, Gracián's awareness of a *culto lector* ("cultured reader") is constant. He addresses him familiarly as "thou" in what seems a casual conversation. Porqueras-Mayo[32] notes a symbolic analogy between the *book* and the *reader* when Gracián exclaims:

> And you, O Book, although what is new and tasteful might guarantee you the good will if not the praise of your readers, you may hope for the good fortune of coming across someone who understands you. (p. 81; 234b)

When our critic addresses the reader, he seems to take upon himself the responsibility of directing the intellectual life of the latter by calling to his attention particular ideas. For instance, he advises the reader to buy Juan Rufo's *Seiscientos apoftegmas:* (600 Maxims) "get it, for it is a book of good pleasure (p. 254; 234b)." Other instances[33] of this preoccupation for the reader include the following:

> read, reread, respect, and perhaps remarvel at this Spanish epigram on a fountain, which don Manuel de Salinas . . . imparts to us from the source of his perennial imagination. (p. 254; 290a)

> Proof lies in this extremely perfect sonnet (a poem never sufficiently appreciated) by don Miguel de Ribellas. (p. 275; 296a)

> Read it, for it is one of the books of good taste and great interest, worthy of the choicest library. (Reference is to the *Dichos memorables* [Memorable Sayings] of Giovanni Botero, p. 485; 368b).

Moreover, Gracián is attracted to examples of poetry which address the reader directly, such as in some Latin poems of Martial and Andrelinus.

Besides a concern for the reader, other dominant themes of the baroque period are emphasized in *The Mind's Wit*. Gracián refers to grotesque themes, death, sorrow, metamorphosis and those dealing with mordant humor and satire. He has a strong interest in time and shows how man is caught in the violent contrast between the temporal and the eternal. The element of time, therefore, is an important point of reference for writing: "In the variableness of time, past and present, may be pondered the contrast of circumstances" (p. 140; 254b).

His citations of mythological themes reveal the seventeenth-century practice of using mythology for the decoration of art, as opposed to its possibly more integral role in early Renaissance literature. For instance, allusions to classical mythology enhance and decorate literary expression: "Allusions, with their enigmatic framework, seem to mimic the dictation and subtlety of the angels" (p. 731; 449a).

The words "bizarre," "ornate," "extravagant," and "distorted" are frequently used to define aspects of literature throughout *The Mind's Wit*. Gracián especially emphasizes the words "disequilibrium" in style and "disillusionment" as descriptive of the writer's art and intention. Disillusionment in themes is useful, because it makes the reader *see* disenchantment in life:

This device may be called cautionary because, just as the sun lights the hemisphere, so these principles illuminate the reason with their grave and prudent disillusionment. (p. 674; 431b)

Disequilibrium in style, meanwhile, creates dramatic and shocking effects in order to produce awe and wonder in the reader.

The grotesque elements apparent in baroque literature are achieved by many devices. In *The Mind's Wit* Gracián asserts that disturbance and tension are created by means of destruction of syntax, wordplay, ingenious puns, and violent contrasts. Gracián anticipates Wylie Sypher's view of the baroque[34] as a form of release and fulfillment:

When the material of the original remark is great, it entreats the mind to run on and on until it is not content with one nor with two releases, but multiplies its daring solutions. (p. 202; 275a)

Much of the literature of the baroque deals with impressions and dreams which enhance reality by distortion, giving freedom to the writer's ideas. For Gracián, dreams offer the writer a world of limitless, imaginative creation: "In the matter of dreams, there have been rare and extravagant interpretations drawn about what the things dreamed of signified" (p. 631; 418b).

Another aspect of the baroque aesthetic is the disunity of the parts and the unity of the whole in a literary work. Gracián dwells on this point in his discussion:

Compound wit consists of many acts and principal parts, while they are unified in the moral, artful framework of a discourse. Each stone among the precious ones, taken for itself, might compete with a star; but many set together on some little trinket seem capable of emulating the firmament, a cunning composition of the imagination in which a sublime structure is erected, not of columns and architraves, but of subject matter and conceits. (pp.110—11; 245a)

Spanish baroque literature has been described as obscure and difficult, didactically oriented as a result of the Counter-Reformation.[35] It is this type of literature that Gracián describes and prescribes in *The Mind's Wit*. As previously observed, he particularly prefers the hermetic art of Góngora and the didactic art of Martial or Mateo Alemán.

Curtius has defined the baroque as abnormal or mannerist expression.[36] Gracián is constant in his search for the unique and abnormal in literary writing. In *The Mind's Wit* Gracián urges the writer to employ syntactic gymnastics in order to play with the language, that is, to achieve sarcastic and paradoxical thoughts, equivocal meanings, and profound ideas.

Baroque aesthetics sought the infinite. Artists, not being content with the world of ugliness, longed for a world of purity and spirituality. Gracián extends this idea in that many of his literary examples are concerned with religious sentiments and ideas. He praises those poets who have dealt with divine thoughts — Lope de Vega, Góngora, and Marino. He also recommends the religious sermon as a notable literary form because it produces and focuses upon reality and disillusionment.

Dualism is a feature of the baroque theory, and Gracián treats both the profane and the popular in literary expression. Referring to the tradition of *a lo divino* ("divine accommodation") in Spanish literature,[37] Gracián suggests that "when a text from secular learning is adjusted to holy matters, it must be sublime and on a worthwhile subject" (pg. 578; 403a).

This idea is underlined further in his many selections of poetry in which the profane subject matter and manner of expression reflect divine thoughts. In addition, he appreciated the extravagant intrigues of baroque dramatists like Lope de Vega and Calderón de la Barca, and praises the bizarre (i.e., marvelous, unusual) and inventive spirit of Guillén de Castro. Most important is Gracián's recognition of a characteristic of the baroque which Wölfflin has defined as "open form."[38] Our critic describes the meaning of the literary work as relative:

It sometimes happens that the correspondence and conformity between the subject compared and the term used in the comparison are not exact, and then the course of thought is either simply ended or pressed on conditionally. (p. 294; 302b)

Other devices which emphasize Gracián's feeling for baroque literature are his stated preference for the superabundance of conceits, paradoxes, contrasts, surprises, entangled plots, enigma, and mystery. Especially striking is his concept of the panoramic effect attained by the epic form.

An important question is, Why did Gracián refer to and describe religious moralizing in secular Spanish literature? Certainly, as a Jesuit, he probably supports to some degree the mandates of the Council of Trent (1545–1563), which discerned the chaotic and fleeting nature of the contradictory world.[39] Sharing such a world view, Gracián adhered to the utilitarian doctrine for literature because he viewed the experience of the world as, from the point of view of man, a temporary and tormented circumstance. The yearning for immortality in literary creation, such as conceived by Gracián, and again indicative of baroque aesthetics, manifests itself in cleverness of thought, conceptismo, and cleverness of language, culteranismo. The result of these ideas is a complex and extravagant literature which veils the intense internal struggle as experienced by Gracián and the seventeenth-century writers in Spain as well as in Europe.

It has been observed, then, that Gracián evaluates and describes the main tendencies of the literary practices of his age. His ideas bespeak the ingredients of baroque aesthetics—he did not categorize or systematize them because his ideas tend to be casual remarks from which emerge a comprehension of language and literature. Versatile and, as many think, the best critic of his time, Gracián excels in transcribing and preserving the unique characteristics of a tumultuous literary period.

V   *Conclusion*

Chapters 2 and 3 have attempted to show why *The Mind's Wit* has been and continues to be a notable contribution to Spanish literary theory, an outstanding contribution to baroque aesthetics. Its significance may be summarized as follows: (1) *The Mind's Wit* develops a new aesthetic theory based on agudeza, ingenio and concepto; (2) the treatise is the only major work in seventeenth-century Spanish literature which undertakes a detailed study of wit; (3) Gracián advances a concept of poetry that breaks with Aristotelian imitation in order to emphasize the role of creation in poetry; (4) an evaluation of the aspects of literary composition indicates Gracián's wide range of literary ideas; and (5) the author's distinguished compendium of literary preferences provides insights into literature on universal, national, and regional levels.

CHAPTER 4

The Master Critic: *Forms and Themes*

I *Introduction*

MAN'S allegorical journey as expressed in Western literature recalls numerous titles: Homer's *Odyssey*, Virgil's *Aeneid*, Dante's *Divine Comedy*, Bunyan's *Pilgrim's Progress*, and Spenser's *Faerie Queen*, among others. In the literature of seventeenth-century Spain, Quevedo's *Sueños* (Dreams) and Gracián's *Criticón* (The Master Critic[1]) represent the culminating works of this particular fictional mode. Generally speaking, allegory by itself has served men of letters to explain moral, spiritual, and natural truths concerning the human condition. It is a way of expressing in the material terms of every-day experience abstract or transcendental concepts which otherwise might lie beyond the reader's grasp. The form has served both spiritual and social needs, and its function includes education (i.e., recognition of the meaning of the allegorical figures) as well as entertainment (i.e., delight over the ingeniousness of the figures). More specifically, the journey motif of Everyman, the *topos* of the *homo viator* who undertakes the great adventure, and experiences the dangers, of life along the metaphorical highways of the world, has provided the narrative framework for several works, *The Master Critic* included.

Although all literature can be called allegorical in the sense that it is metaphoric of human experience, it is valuable to stress allegory as a particular, or a more narrowly defined, modality of premodern literature. To seek out differences between a work like the famous *Lazarillo de Tormes* and *The Master Critic* is instructive. The former is quasi-naturalistic in that throughout the stages of the journey of life, there are abstract values but there is also, to be sure, the narrative attempt to give the impression of day-to-day life. *The Master Critic*, however, is quite abstract and nonnaturalistic in its narrative elaboration. For example, it uses the common allegorical procedure of personification (the embodiment of abstract concepts, usually virtues and vices, in the forms of persons whose only function is to *personify* those qualities—by extension, animals and monsters may also be used). Also, in the movement from incident to incident, no intrinsic anecdotal justification is given, nor is there more than a purely abstract correspondence with day-to-day experience. (Of course, this does not mean that the work does not deal with profound human experience but only that the latter is identified and presented in nonnaturalistic terms.) In *The Master Critic* all of these elements—nonnaturalistic development, use of stereotyped personifications, as well as widely recognizable mythological figures—are part of the identification of the work as allegory in the specialized sense.

The Master Critic is not only Gracián's longest and most mature work (it was written over a period of six years and published in three different parts in 1651, 1653, and 1657), but it is also his only work of fiction. The novel is an interesting piece of literature, rich in imagery, vocabulary, moral philosophy, classical mythology, imaginative visions, complicated allegorical conceits, and abstract ideas. Its art is thoroughly complicated; its length is awesome. Indeed, Gracián can hardly be said to have followed his own famous dictum of brevity. In short, his work is a summa of social criticism, a compendium of almost all the literary and moral thought to be found in his previous writings. It is a splendid example of the baroque *Gesamtkunstwerk*. Published in defiance of his superiors and a source of antagonism and ill-will between the author and his order, *The Master Critic* is nothing more nor less than an allegory of life, both as a general human circumstance and as a seventeenth-century European reality. On the one hand, it is an encomium of the individualism of man and, on the other, a severe censure of man's behavior and of Gracián's own times.

Unfortunately, although the book has become a Spanish classic, it no longer enjoys the wide reading public it once had. In the nineteenth century, Schopenhauer, who shared the pessimism of Gracián, declared that *The Master Critic* is one of the best books in the world. As an alternate opinion from the twentieth century, the

Argentine poet Jorge Luis Borges totally repudiates Gracián as a
man and as an artist:

BALTASAR GRACIÁN[2]

Labyrinth, quibbles, emblems,
Such bleak laborious minutiae
Were all this Jesuit knew of poetry,
Which he had reduced to stratagems.

No music in his soul; but this inane
Herbarium of metaphors and punning
And a veneration of cunning
And contempt for the human and superhuman.

Homer's ancient voice he never heard,
Or the voice—silver and moonlight—of Virgil;
Nor saw Oedipus the accursed in exile
Nor Christ who is dying on a piece of board.

The stars, the radiant eastern stars
That is the vast aurora slowly fade,
Of these he blasphemously said
Chickens of the celestial acres.

As ignorant of divine love he was
As of that other burning in the bone;
The Pale One surprised him one afternoon
As he was reading El Marino's stanzas.

His later destiny is not given;
The dust that yesterday was his frame
Loosened to the changes of the tainted grave,
The soul of Gracián rose up to heaven.

What did he feel then contemplating plainly
The Archetypes and the Splendors?
Perhaps he cried and told himself: Vainly
I sought nourishment in shadows and errors.

What happened when the relentless

Sun of God, The Truth, put forth its fire?
Maybe the light of God left him blind there
In the center of the endless heavens.

I know another ending. Doped on his themes
Infinitesimal, Gracián never noticed heaven
And turns over in his memory as ever
Labyrinths, quibbles and emblems.

(Translated by Irving Feldman)

II   *General Characteristics*

The plan of the novel, although not original in its broad outlines, is unique and significant in terms of theme, structure and philosophy. It is a philosophic-didactic compendium consisting of thirty-eight rambling chapters which recount the travels, adventures, and misadventures of Critilo, the archetype of intellect and reason, and Andrenio, the archetype of instinct and passion. Together the two characters can be said to constitute in a complementary sense the totality of man's nature. Throughout the novel, both are spokesmen on a variety of subjects. The two protagonists, like Dante, and many another "lost traveler," are led by a series of guides who are both mythological and allegorical figures in their journey through life in order to find Felisinda, who personifies happiness, and in order to become *personas* (i.e., truly persons). In their wanderings, which are very much reminiscent of the more naturalistic picaresque mode in Renaissance and baroque fiction, they go from the Island of Santa Elena to Madrid, Castilla, Aragón, the Pyrenees, France, Picardy, Germany, the Alps, Italy, and Rome, finally ending up on the Island of Immortality. Together they experience all kinds of difficulties and perils. But in spite of their misfortunes and disillusionments, they manage to attain self-perfection. And although the tone of *The Master Critic* is strongly pessimistic and misanthropic, Gracián does present an exit for man: an immortality based on artistic, political, social, and cultural achievements.

Obviously Gracián had read widely and had absorbed the many literary influences of his day. For example, Menéndez y Pelayo has been able to discover an oriental influence in *The Master Critic;*[3] José Montesinos regards the novel as a picaresque creation;[4] Romera

Navarro emphasizes the Byzantine elements of the work.[5] What a balance sheet of the historical investigations on the novel shows is that it is an amalgam of Oriental, classical, and Western literary traditions, with Oriental apologues, descriptive narration, moral and philosphic digressions, allegorical conceits, picaresque wanderings, circumstantial exempla, social criticism, and satire. Although it is generally believed that Gracián's knowledge of Greek is secondhand, he is, however, able to make many allusions to Greek writers with whose work he is familiar: Homer, Aesop, Heliodorus, Lucian, Aristotle, Plato, Sophocles, Euripides, Aristophanes, and Plutarch.

Likewise, the influence of Latin writers on *The Master Critic* is overwhelming. From Cicero and Seneca Gracián has taken the sententious maxims and literary modes of moral intent. He does not surpass them in profundity of thought, but he does excel them in conciseness of style and conceptual rapidity. Horace, Ovid, and Virgil are the poets who have left their mark on Gracián, while he also shares an attitude of bitter satire with Martial, Persius, and Juvenal. The humor and fresh spirit of the New Comedy of Plautus and Terence are also evident throught the novel. And the philosophy of historians like Pliny, Tacitus, Caesar, and Suetonius permeates Gracián's thinking. Romera Navarro is one literay historian who has emphasized the unusual importance of the Roman world in *The Master Critic*.[6]

Throughout his writings, Gracián's theory of conduct for the ideal man centers on prudence and reason. This theory is sustained in *The Master Critic*, where man himself has become the vehicle through the allegorical framework for conveying the Jesuit's ideas. In order to capture the spirit of the work, it is essential to place it within the frame of reference of the baroque and the Counter-Reformation in Spain, a time when the organization of knowledge was based on complex dualities, counterpoints, ambivalences, and opposites.

In *The Master Critic* symmetry, totality, and harmony function not as complementary terms but rather as opposites. This constant tension is developed through the interplay of the two protagonists, who discover life in opposite ways, see reality in different perspectives, and think antithetically. Together, however, they form a total human personality, and together theirs is the quest for identification, happiness, and fulfillment. The following list of characteristics associated with each demonstrates the dialectical nature of the two characters; the complexity of the novel rests on the allegorical depiction of their antithetical yet complementary nature:

Critilo	*Andrenio*
Intellectual	Emotive
Mature	Immature, inexperienced
Independent, self-reliant	Dependent, unreliable
Stoic	Epicurean
Teacher	Pupil
Father	Son
Perspicacious	Gullible
Introvert	Extrovert
Spiritual	Corporal
Quiet	Noisy

Antonio Prieto has discussed this duality as the structural justification of the work:

The meeting of shipwrecked Critilo with Andrenio on the Island of Santa Elena will be the meeting of human duality, in which reason and prudence blend with nature and imprudent generosity to form the human totality, the main actor of the narrative. It is a synthesis of two halves whose analysis and separation Gracián uses to show that mixture of opposites which dualizes the narrative subject and which ends in a synthesis with Gracián's incorporation of the individual in his composition as a person. The subject is dualized in this fashion in an allegorical play of synthesis-analysis-synthesis, which in the Baroque mode of contrasts is going to point out the composition of opposites which govern existence in their travels across the "stage" of the world. In his development, the narrative subject will be portrayed by a narrative form rich in opposites and tied to the technique of counterpoint which will resort expressively to the frequent use of antithesis, oxymoron, and homonymy. It is a perfect gauging of the narrative subject to the word, which under conceptism, structures *The Master Critic* in a tight correspondence of all its elements.[7]

III   *Narrative Organization*

The first-time reader of *The Master Critic*, which is a highly imaginative as well as an extravagantly diffuse work, is astounded by Gracián's busy world, populated with hosts of both real and imaginary characters, many of the latter grotesque. This narrative world is further enriched by the accumulation of allegories, ideas, events, commentaries, and elaborate and sustained puns. In the introductory remarks to his reader, Gracián announces the moral purpose of his all-encompassing, baroque *Gesamtkunstwerk:*

He procurado juntar lo seco de la filosofía con lo entretenido de la invención, lo picante de la sátira con lo dulce de la épica. . . . Comienzo por la hermosa Naturaleza, paso a la primoroso Arte y paro en la útil Moralidad. (I, 519).

I have attempted to join the dryness of philosophy with the entertainment of invention, the piquant of satire with the sweetness of the epic. . . . Beginning with fair Nature, I move on to elegant Art, and I end up with useful Morality.

From the outset, the author establishes the static, moral backdrop of the novel.

In order to understand the relationship between Gracián's moral goals and the diffuse narrative of *The Master Critic*, a detailed summary of the work is presented below. (The Roman numeral before a paragraph refers to the individual chapter, called *Crisi* by Gracián)[8]

Part One: Youth

I.   The ill-fated Critilo is washed ashore on the Island of Santa Elena and is saved by a young savage. Critilo names the latter Andrenio (meaning the "natural man" in Greek), teaches him to speak, and undertakes the long process of educating him. Andrenio relates his previous life in a dark cave (earth's womb), sustained by wild beasts.

II.   Andrenio emotionally proclaims the glories of his discovery of God's brilliant theater of the universe when he is freed from his prison by an earthquake which ruptures the cave. He perceives the world with sensitivity and freshness and is overwhelmed by all of nature and the cosmos.

III.   In a eulogy of god and the natural order, Andrenio continues to be fascinated by earth and life, while Critilo endeavors to intellectualize his companion's perceptual sensations.

IV.   Critilo begins to confess his labyrinthine past, saying that he was reared among men, man's worst enemy. His story is interrupted when a boat comes, and the pair set sail for Spain. During the voyage, Critilo tells his life story: his irresponsible youth in Goa, his love affair with Felisinda, and his ruin when he kills a rival suitor. In prison, he undergoes maturation, cultivating the arts and sciences, especially moral philosophy. Time passes until one day Felisinda requests him to come to Spain. En route, Critilo is robbed of his jewels and shoved overboard by the captain, to be rescued by Andrenio.

V.   Upon arriving in Spain and "entering the world," they witness the sight of unruly children pursued and devoured by bestial passion and Bad Tendencies. Reason rescues several of the children and gives the pair her touchstone. At the crossroads of life, Critilo and Andrenio avoid extremes by choosing the oath of the Golden Mean.

VI.   The centaur Chiron, connoisseur of the world, shows the travelers a global view of the depressing state of the century, a period lacking in eminent men. At the Plaza Mayor, Madrid's central square, they view the vices of humanity and the "world turned upside down," a world filled with injustices, social inequities, corrupt politicians, bad judges and doctors, opportunistic soldiers, and irresponsible writers. Andrenio, disenchanted, wishes to return to his previous "natural" existence, but Critilo advises him that man's only recourse is to continue to live intensely.

VII.   Chiron offers the pair counsel: they must understand things other than as they appear. Proteus, now their guide (he is a treacherous one), takes them to the Palace of *Falsimundo* ("False World"). They first pass by the Fountain of Deceits, whose sought-after waters indicate the unreliability of the senses, and then by the City of Deceit and the Plaza of the *Vulgo* ("Mobs") where a demagogic politician—an attack on Machiavelli—seduces the masses. At the Banquet of Deceits, they witness the tragicomedy of Everyman's plight in the world. Andrenio foolishly enters

Falsimundo's palace and is imprisoned.

VIII.   The wonders and magic of Artemia, Queen of Science, are numerous, and she even sends a sage to rescue Andrenio from the terrible Falsimundo, the monster who represents all the paragons of vice.

IX.   Andrenio tells Artemia that the greatest of creations is man himself. The two and Andrenio engage in a philosophic, moral discourse concerning the nature of man as seen through his anatomy. Meanwhile, Falsimundo, enraged with jealousy, joins Envy in inciting the masses to persecute Artemia.

X.   Artemia outwits the raging mob and escapes to Toledo. At the Inn of Pleasure, Critilo chooses books while Andrenio opts for flowers. Andrenio foolishly enters the Inn and again his mentor must rescue him with the aid of an old sage.

XI.   Before departing, the sage relates an allegory concerning Good and Evil and man's love for the latter. A courtier suggests that Homer's *Odyssey* is the best of all possible guidebooks, for from it they can learn to dodge forthcoming perils and evils. At court, they feel alienated, until Critilo wins friends with his jewels. Even Adrenio receives a message from a supposed cousin.

XII.   *Falsirena* ("False Siren") reveals that Andrenio's mother Felisinda was secretly married in Goa and gave birth to a child whom she left on the island in care of Divine Providence. Andrenio rushes to tell Critilo that they are indeed father and son. Falsirena tells the two, however, that Felisinda is in Germany; Critilo entrusts his jewels to her and goes off to the Escorial and Aranjuez. Upon returning, Egenio, his guide with six senses, helps to free Andrenio from the Cave of Lust.

XIII.   At the great Fair of the World in the Plaza of Convenience, the protagonists discover all the virtues necessary to aid them in becoming true persons, and they discover also all the vices that relate to materialism and the flesh. Critilo and his son acquire the greatest truth: "the truly wise man, the man who has himself and God, has all that he needs." They then proceed to Aragón, the abode of maturity.

Part Two: Maturity

I.   Argus is one of the guards at the bustling Customs House of Life where each person is examined for the moral, spiritual, intellectual, or physical reforms necessary for the age of maturity. Critilo and Andrenio listen to a reading of the Laws of Wisdom that lead men "to be persons." Argus then bathes the two in a magic potion which provides them with perspicacity and sensitivity.

II. Argus presents the pair with a great overview of life, a fusion of times past and present (the ancients excel while the moderns are inferior), the great nations, the marvels of Rome, Toledo, and Paris. In Huesca the two enjoy a tour of Salastano's museum with all its collections of wondrous treasures.

III. The mythological character Gerión and the protagonists eulogize the glories of true friendship and discuss the nature of Spain and the Spanish temperament. Later a wily Frenchman deceives the two travelers and they end up imprisoned in the Dungeon of Gold populated by human passions and ruled by the monster Avarice.

IV. Freed by the "Winged Man," Critilo and Andrenio agree to follow him to the Palace of *Sofisbella* ("Wisdom"). Since Andrenio, however, chooses to join the ignorant activities of the masses, Critilo and his guide go on to enjoy the eternal intellectual and spiritual joys of men in Sofisbella's magnificent museum, which contains a world of books. Such characters as Poetry, History, Time, Memory and Truth address Critilo and lead him through the various salons.

V. Meanwhile, in the Main Plaza of the Universe, Andrenio, accompanied by Cecrops, witnesses the Bedlam produced by the mobs of noisy fools, half men, half animals. The latter engage in counterproductive activities such as war, idle chatter, inefficient government, and petty squabbles. Andrenio is frightened by the sight of the monstrous Vulgacho (i.e., "ugly mob") and begs to return to Critilo.

VI. A dwarf advises Critilo to stop searching for the physical presence of Sofisbella: she is in heaven but continues to live on earth through books. He then takes Critilo to Fortune's House, where he joins Andrenio. Together they see the defense of Fortune against those mortals who attack her. At Fortune's Table the travelers opt for truth; immediately Time, Death, and others close in on the crowds.

VII. This time Happiness saves the pair. At the Convent of Hypocrisy their attention is drawn to the many hypocrites cloaked in the guise of virtue and religion—an anticlerical satire. They meet

Hipocrinda, "all body and no spirit," who praises the life of "no ser [virtuoso] y parecerlo (not being virtuous but appearing to be so)."

VIII.   Upon leaving France, the two meet Bravery, who takes them to the Museum of Bravery, where they are armed with all the symbolical weapons of bravery—truth, light, prudence, and a generous heart. There follows a discussion of the dominant characteristics of each nation, as well as references to brave contemporary leaders and historical feats.

IX.   At the Amphitheater of Monstrosities, Critilo and Andrenio, now protected by Keenness, view the masses wallowing in vices: feigned courtesy, false honor, adultery, and ambition. The principal monsters of the World, the Flesh and Satan, fight to control mortals, but all the former are appeased by dividing the kingdom among themselves.

X.   Guided by *Lucindo* ("prodigious with light"), the pair make the arduous trip through forested and mountainous terrain to reach the Palace of Virtue. They reach the celestial summit where they admire Virtue's beauty and her justice in dealing with mankind. She makes Critilo and Andrenio candidates for Felisinda, the personification of Happiness.

XI.   After having crossed the Bridge of Buts, the pair enter the Court of Honor. Here they find beautiful buildings with roofs of glass shattered by the stone-throwing Momo. A quarrel ensues between him and his counterpart *Bobo* ("Simpleton"), but the travelers are carried off by another marvel with the promise to lead them to the Kingdom of true honor.

XII.   The marvel turns out to be *El Asombrado* ("Shadow Man") who guides them to the Throne of Command, where they engage in a discussion on politics. *El Extremado* ("the Man of Extremes") tells them that man is really unwilling to accept the responsibility to rule and to lead. Critilo and Andrenio ask him to lead them to Felisinda.

XIII.   The two learn that the true sovereignty of man is to be sovereign of himself. Their adventures include an encounter with Envy at the *Jaula de Todos* ("the Cage of All Men"), where several of the mad inmates begin to assail the travelers. They are rescued by El Extremado when he blows the horn of truth. Now the two must undertake the journey of old age.

Part Three: Old Age

I. In the white, barren and sad landscape of the Alps, the pair find themselves experiencing Old Age. She is different for each man: a cruel hag for Andrenio, whereas for Critilo she appears as a dignified figure.

II. Old Age bestows titles upon the travelers: Andrenio is *viejo* ("old man") and Critilo is *senior* ("sir"). *Don Fulano de la Lengua Horadada* ("Mr. So and So with the Pierced Tongue"), an inveterate gossiper, invites them to the Palace of Happiness located in Germany, the place of sheer intoxication. Andrenio becomes drunk—a defense and condemnation of wine ensues—and Critilo confronts the untidy Queen of Drunkenness, who is the source of all evils, especially for the aged. She belches out several sordid monsters: Heresy, Avarice, Envy, the Furies, and the Sirens,

III. Critilo and his new friend, *El Acertador* ("the Correct Guesser"), save Andrenio from his drunken stupor, and the three set out for Italy; Germany has proved a haven for heretics and drunks. The three meet the masses who have dismissed Truth from the world and put Lie on the throne. Truth has also given birth to a horrible son, Hatred.

IV. El Acertador now becomes *El Descifrador* ("the Decipherer"), who advises Critilo to see beyond the superficial reality of life. To *descifrar* is an art, an art which allows man to interpret the book of the world and the book of the heart. The Decipherer demonstrates his rare ability by interpreting the character of those he meets. The various personalities are described in "rhetorical" terms: diphthongs have contradictory personalities; etceteras are the abbreviations for all the evil in man; *qutildeques* (Gracián's neologism for *cualquiera*, "anybody") represent the nondescript anybodies; dots, periods, and tildes are mean of spirit—all appear to be other than what they really are. At the Plaza of the World their guide unmasks the trickeries of a glib charlatan who fabricates a host of lies, deceits and ambiguities.

V. Critilo laments the difficulties of life, only to learn from Zahorí, his new guide, that man himself must accept the guilt for his fallen state. Zahorí, a moralist, *sees* into the depths of man's soul and mind. At the Palace Without Doors, they behold a spectacle of human fraud: loathsome men, street walkers, libelers, gossipers. No one understands anyone, and all refuse to accept knowledge of any kind.

VI.   Zahorí and Critilo save Andrenio from the bedlam of the Palace, and together they journey to the Court of Knowledge. At a crossroads, the protagonists choose separate and antithetical paths: Critilo that of astuteness, a path choked with serpents, and Andrenio, that of simplicity, a path filled with doves. Soon they opt for the road of the Golden Mean where *El Sesudo* ("The Brainy One") is to guide them to their final destination. First they review and praise all the establishments of culture and knowlege. They also listen to the reform of popular sayings and are then taken to a workshop to sharpen their wits.

VII.   Wending their way to Rome, and against the better judgment of El Sesudo, the two interrupt an argument between Sloth and Boastfulness. The former promises a life of pure rest and joy, while the latter guarantees a life of immortality. Boastfulness leads them to the Rooms of Pride, where they contemplate a presumptuous humanity.

VIII.   Sloth proceeds to steer them to his meadow, where the ethic of comfort and laziness have made the inhabitants sybarites and nonpeople. At the Cave of Nothingness, the destination of three-quarters of the world, they are fascinated by the Reform of Books: a strong monster is employed in condemning to nothingness many books of history and literature.

IX.   In Rome the travelers listen to geniuses (Barclay, Boccalini, and others) discuss the meaning of true human happiness. A humble employee interrupts them to say that "true human happiness is found in heaven." The *Cortesano* ("Courtier"), their present guide, informs them that their beloved Felisinda, Andrenio's mother and Critilo's wife, has died and is in heaven. A panegyric to Italy's brilliance follows, whereupon the Courtier promises to give the two companions a panoramic view of time.

X.   By means of the Wheel of Time and the magic of some crystal lenses, Critilo and Andrenio attain insights into the meaning of time and fortune: history repeats itself, the ancients surpass the moderns, and there is nothing new under the sun. Their glimpse into the future includes their own forthcoming demise. The two remain enchanted, as they survey the unwinding thread of life from the divine heavens.

XI.   At another plaza filled with a teeming mob, the two are impressed by a madman who is walking across a tightrope. The Courtier tells them that even more perilous is the slender thread of our own lives. Next they enter the Inn of Life where they come into contact with Death and her court. She orders their death but *El Inmortal* ("Immortality") assures them that there is an escape.

XII.   Man's escape from an ignominious death, of course, consists in being an "eminent man." Their immortal guide takes them in a boat to the marvelous Island of Immortality where all great people—and they are few indeed—live forever through their accomplishments and their cultural contributions. The guard Merit admits the pair to the Museum of Eternity after examining their papers, which prove their worthiness by virtue of an arduous but prudent trip through life.

IV   *Themes*

An examination of *The Master Critic* from a thematic point of view immediately opens up the work for the reader in terms of Gracián's moral goal. In addition to an intricate plot supported by a vast erudition, one finds that the novel contains a multitude of recurring ideas and commentaries voiced by the characters, primarily by the sagacious Critilo, who is the archetypal educator and civilizer of not only Andrenio but of all humanity. We can see how the name of the protagonist bears a direct relationship to the title, *The Master Critic*: Critilo is the critic, the observer, the decipherer, and the interpreter of life—he is, in short, Gracián's literary alter ego in a world of constant discovering, seeing, and telling.

In keeping with baroque and Counter-Reformation thought, the novel probes the nature of the world. For Gracián, the world is a complex system of deceits, an enigma, a labyrinth of lies and ambiguities. What prevails is man's constant battle against *parecer* ("appearance; what seems to be") and *ser* ("what is"). Critilo, like many of the subsidiary guides, counselors, sages, and personifications of wisdom that appear throughout the novel, stresses the importance of *ver* ("seeing"), man's strongest weapon against an otherwise deceptive world. Man is imprisoned within a façade of false appearances and what is needed is an inner eye (as St. Ignatius of Loyola also insisted), a keen perceptivity in order to *see* beyond superficial realities[9] Gracián believes that the real heroes of life do not accept apparent truths but rather pursue profound significant ones. Ver along with *saber* ("knowing") are the principal keys for a worthwhile existence.

Besides the eternal battle between illusion and reality—and it must be remembered that Critilo is repeatedly obliged to explain what Andrenio *really* sees and experiences as they venture through life—man must set as his goal to *ser persona,* to become a person, through rational, prudent activity. In a sense, Gracián liberates human life from a dependence on the supernatural; his consciousness does not primarily focus on God but rather on man, his intellect and reason. It is precisely this concept of *ser* ("being") that is so highly prized by Gracián. After all, *The Master Critic* is man's quest for ser, both in this life and after death, and it is a quest described wholly within a secular, nontheological context.

Clearly, the themes of *The Master Critic* are not faithful to the restrictive prevailing Catholic beliefs, for Gracián's moral precepts do not deal with the religious issues of grace and original sin attributable to his more orthodox contemporaries.[10] That is, the Jesuit deviated from the traditional norm of theocentricity espoused by great literati like Dante, Bunyan, Cervantes, and Calderón, to name a few, whose views of the world are ultimately God-centered. For his day, Gracián is a free and daring soul who set his novel within a pagan, secular world. Critilo speaks infrequently about God and the devil, but he turns to contemplate at length the human condition, its follies, vices, and stupidities. Since *The Master Critic* is not a theocentric work of literature, its author elaborates not on theology but on human behavior, and the major concerns of the composition rest on the latter. Look, for instance, at the allegories which stress secular subjects, such as honor, fortune, valor, all of which constitute substantial principles for this life. Likewise, the events of the characters' journey emphasize man, not religion, while the symbolism in the work follows the same orientation based on nature and myth. Nonetheless, Gracián remains a participant in Counter-Reformation Spain and a proponent of Aristotelian-Thomistic philosophy. Consequently he continues to believe that reason is man's superior faculty and with it he is able to solve his problems and difficulties.

The theme of nature[11] plays an integral role in Gracián's world of fiction, both from a physical point of view in that the protagonists must deal with nature physically and psychologically—they must overcome her many adversities—and from an aesthetic point of view. In the opening chapters, the discussions concerning nature foreshadow somewhat the primitivism of Rousseau, principally in terms of the rustic joys of nature and the innocence of the noble savage as symbolized by Andrenio. The beauty and harmony of nature and the universe are incomparable in their supreme perfection. Nature is viewed as a capricious phenomenon filled with harmonious discords. God is not only the Prime Mover but the consummate artist who has created the world with his own agudeza and ingenio. Moreover, God's art provides man with a supreme means of attaining knowledge:

Sola la infinita subiduría de aquel Supremo Hacedor pudo hallar el modo, el orden y el concierto de tan hermosa y perene variedad. (I, 525)

Only the infinite knowledge of the Supreme Maker could find the way, the order, and the harmony of such a beautiful and perennial variety.

No se ve, pero se conoce y, como soberano príncipe, estando retirado a su inaccesible incomprehensibilidad, nos habla por medio de sus criaturas. Así que con razón definió un filósofo este universo espejo grande de Dios. Mi libro, le llamaba el sabio indocto, donde en cifras de criaturas estudió las divinas perfecciones. (I, 539)

He cannot be seen, but he is known and, like a sovereign prince who is secluded in his inaccessible incomprehensibility, he speaks to us through his creatures. This is how a philosopher so aptly defined this universe, an immense mirror of God. My book, the unlettered wiseman called it, where in ciphers of creatures he studied the divine perfections.

Critilo and his pupil view the cosmos of nature, in typical baroque fashion, as a magnificent theater filled with awesome wonders like celestial time, the starry heavens, the seas, day, and other mysteries. But what brings discord and disorder to this otherwise utopian setting of nature is man, far worse even than the beasts. The *Master Critic* abounds in misanthropic attitudes toward man, who with his prime sin of foolishness perverts, corrupts, and transgresses against nature and the universe. Critilo repeatedly tells

Andrenio that life is a constant battle against evil and, in fact, warns him against man whose morality and corporality are bestial:

> . . . que si los hombres no son fieras es porque son más fieros, que de su crueldad aprendieron muchas veces ellas. Nunca mayor peligro hemos tenido, que ahora que estamos entre ellos. (I, 542)

for if men are not beasts it is because the more beastly for the former have often learned from the cruelty of the latter. We have never been in greater danger than we are now among these latter.

> Créeme que no hay lobo, no hay león, no hay tigre, no hay basilisco que llegue al hombre; a todos exede en fiereza. (I, 543)

Believe me when I say that there is no wolf, no lion, no tiger, no basilisk that can touch man; he exceeds them all in his ferocity.

However, man is nonetheless capable of understanding truth and beauty through artistic and abstract expression. Thus man, who possesses a complex duplicity, figures simultaneously as both the destroyer of harmony and nature and as the Maker who through Will can direct his intellectual and artistic energies to restoring to nature its beauty and balance.

As is well known, *The Master Critic* has the distinction of being unrelentingly pessimistic in affirming that life is a constant death, man is bad, and society is irremediably corrupt. Basically it is man himself who is the theme of *The Master Critic*, man who is defined and redefined within the network of infinite situations and possibilities open to human conduct and behavior. In his departure from scholastic ideas, Gracián believes that man does not fall by birth from Christian grace. Rather, he willfully and stupidly chooses evil in order to satisfy his natural propensity for baser needs and desires. It is significant that during their travels, Critilo and his guides reject all that is physical and carnal as highly repugnant. Man, however, can be redeemed, not by divine redemption, but by human achievement. The highest moral good in Gracián's work is *ser hombre, ser persona*, "to be a man, to be a person." The novel does not shape a traditional, didactic vision of heaven or hell as a reward or punishment for man. Rather man's reward, the culmination of human happiness, lies in fame, in an immortality and an eternal life through posterity, whereas damnation consists of an existence in eternal oblivion. Critilo's and Andrenio's final destination strikes a secular and intellectual note. They end up on the Island of Immortality because the two have fulfilled their destiny as *personas*, having subjugated all of their passions through reason and the use of the Golden Mean, the principle of moderation so esteemed by pre-Christian and Christian moralists alike.

V *Contemporary Commonplaces*

The preceding details can only serve to provide a comprehensive trajectory of the thematic framework of the narrative. In addition, every page of *The Master Critic* offers the reader a didactic medley of ideas and advice. Some of the most significant motifs include the following *topoi*, "commonplaces."

Misogyny. Like Quevedo, Gracián maligns women, who are the frequent targets of his hostility and criticism. Critilo is the major spokesman of Gracián's misogyny, for he has suffered severe trauma because of Felisinda, who, besides representing the embodiment of happiness, is the *belle dame sans merci*. Critilo repeatedly warns Andrenio about feminine treachery. He is clearly antimarriage (wives imprison men) and often blames the shocking condition of the world on woman, the Pandora of all evils. And although, like Felisinda, several women figures, both real and fictitious, are portrayed as aesthetically or intellectually pleasing, many are physically and spiritually repulsive, grotesquely presented as fat and ugly hags, liars, hypocrites, and monsters.

Journey of Life. This topic provides the narrative structure of the work which represents Everyman's peregrination through life in search of *desengaño* ("undeluded truth"). The protagonists follow a linear progression as they engage in activities corresponding to the chronological stages of age.

Theatrum mundi. For Critilo and Andrenio the whole celestial and terrestrial world is a stage where men, as the principal actors, reach awareness, knowledge, and possible self-perfection. The world as a theater, filled with conflict and deceit, also emerges as a place of marvels and intellectual pleasures. The novel also views life as a play with a natural beginning, middle and end.

Complaint on Death. Gracián's eschatological concerns climax in the Cave of Death, where Death appears as a leveler—"all men must die"—of humanity. Death, from her horrible throne of cadavers, somewhat pathetically complains of her experiences with mortals who neither understand nor accept her.

Criticism of Clergy and Monastic Life. In the allegorical episode on the Wasteland of Hipocrinda, Gracián boldly denounces the fraud and hypocrisy of the religious life. Hipocrinda's house (she is the personification of Hypocrisy) actually emerges as a convent whose members lead an epicurean life of carnality and vice under the guise of holiness and virtue. By means of fiction, Gracián covertly satirizes and censures the spiritual licentiousness of the times.

Ubi sunt. Many characters reiterate a disillusionment with the affairs of the world, especially those related to Spain. Consequently there is a yearning for the glories, triumphs, and successful men of times past and a longing for such deeds and magnificence of spirit to return once again to Spain and elsewhere:

que no este siglo de hombres; digo, aquellos de otros tiempos. ¿Qué? ¿Pensábais hallar ahora un don Alonso del Magnánimo en Italia, un Gran Capitán en España, un Enrico Cuarto en Francia. . .? Ya no hay tales héroes en el mundo, ni aun memoria dellos. (I, 561)

for this is not the century of man—that is, of those of other times. What? Did you expect to find now a don Alonso the Magnanimous in Italy, a Great Captain in Spain, a Henry IV in France. . .? There are no longer heroes such as these in the world, nor any recollection of them.

¿. . . volverá al mundo otro Alejandro Magno, un Trajano y el gran Teodosio? ¡Gran cosa sería! (III, 975)

Will another Alexander the Great come into the world, a Trajano and the great Theodosius? That would be a great thing!

Fortune even laments the scarcity of wise people—there are not even two wise persons in one kingdom while *necios*, "fools," are infinite in number.

Continuity. Especially in The Wheel of Time adventure the characters gain insights into the meaning of time as an omnipresent feature of reality. Through the magic of the Courier, they become aware of a fixed cosmic hierarchy, and the circular nature of time;

likewise they see that history repeats itself among a web of ambiguities and that there is a pattern of eternal return. Time is interpreted as continuity with an alternation of highs and lows in temporal events. Closely paralleling this concept throughout *The Master Critic* lies the system of correspondences in the universe: between the animal world and the human world, nature and life, fable and reality, past, present and future times, the microcosm of man and the macrocosm of God, harmony and strife.

Vulgo. Gracián, an elitist, censures the masses as mindless, ignorant, and insensitive creatures who have no destiny to fulfill in this life or in the next. Critilo shuns them for their capriciousness, mediocrity, and lack of imagination (for example, they replace Truth with Lie), and Gracián unmercifully satirizes their absurdity frequently in the work. Approximately three-quarters of humanity belongs to the mob of monsters who march across the pages of *The Master Critic* like the characters of a painting by Hieronymus Bosch. The *vulgo* is defined in these terms by El Sabio:

vulgo no es otra cosa que una sinagoga de ignorantes presumidos y que hablan más de las cosas cuanto menos las entienden. (II, 731)

the masses are nothing but a synagogue of pretentious ignoramuses who, the less they understand of things, the more they speak of them.

Contempt of the World. Incisive invectives against the world and its deceits fill *The Master Critic*. Critilo explains that the world is essentially man's prison, where he is subjected to physical pain and sickness, spiritual unrest, and sorrow, with death as the final punishment and loss. Man is born crying, lives in a theater of tragedies, and dies miserably. Gracián revolts against the senses, carnal love, selfishness, and ambition, because they all highlight this virtually existential condition.

Scorn for the Court. Gracián regards the city as the den of iniquity—the wise and the godly have left for the natural life, while the beasts have come to the cities to become courtiers.

Sin duda que los pocos hombres que habían quedado se han retirado a los montes . . . por no ver lo que en el mundo pasa, y que las fieras se han venido a las ciudades y se han hecho cortesanos. (I, 563)

Without a doubt the few men that were left have retired to the mountains
. . . in order not to see what is happening in the world, and the beasts have
come down to the cities and have become courtiers.

Life in the court is portrayed as a microcosm of all the evils that
exist in the world at large: extravagant, vain women and idle, stupid
men who pursue a life of pleasure as parasites of society. Grand
women are, in reality, adulterous, while great lords are cowards who
pervert honor. (One will recall that the court presented major
problems for seventeenth-century Spanish society.)

Boy and Old Man. The wise and older Critilo helps Andrenio to
acquire maturity and an understanding of life: theirs is a parent-
child relationship both figuratively and literally. At the start,
Andrenio has practically no knowledge of life, but an active
participation in life, with its attendant sensations and experiences,
have enriched him and made him a person.

Letter Writing. The epistolary style is considered to be the
greatest science. For example, Luis Vives's book *De conscribendis
epistolis,* the *Arte de escribir cartas,* (Art of Letter Writing) is cited
as the magnum opus in the quarrel between the arts and science.
During this quarrel it is also decided that men with great
imagination choose natural philosophy (Plato) while men of
prudent judgment are interested by ethics (Seneca).

Landscapes. Atmospheric scenery is often drawn throughout the
novel: there are many descriptions centering on the sea, violent
landscapes, sinister storms, flowers, greenery, steep hills, mountain
grottoes, caves, forests, the sea, meadows, the figurative Alps of Old
Age, and the Island of Immortality. In *The Master Critic* Gracián
associates geography with age, which he sees as a steady
progression upward: youth is spent in the lower, flowery regions
(springtime), middle age along the steep, less verdant hills
(autumn), and finally, old age high up in the region of the Alps
(winter).

Book of Nature, Book of the World. Countless are the times that
the commonplace of the book as a symbol of the universe is used.
Gracián accords the Book of Nature—that is, the experiences of
life—the superior ranking. In the same vein, however, great
writings and books nourish man's spirit and intellect. The Palace of
Sofisbella, of wisdom personified, as well as Salastano's Museum (in

real life the house and library of Gracián's friend and patron Lastanosa), are kingdoms of knowledge for mankind.

The World Upside Down. Corruption and decadence beset Spain in a topsy-turvy world full of chaos and values in reverse. Man has perverted natural laws like honor and virtue. Lies replace truth, vanity and a youthful appearance are treasured values, women rule the world and men, wars predominate, and passions enslave humanity, for which lying, cheating, and malice are the standard norms of life. Materialism is rampant and laziness and idleness are the great ethics.

Censure of the Times.

—¿En cuál [siglo] pensáis vivir, en el del oro o en el del lodo?—Yo diría—respondió Critilo—que en el de hierro. Con tantos [yerros], todo anda errando en el mundo y todo al revés, si ya no es de bronce, que es peor, con tanto cañón y bombarda, todo ardiendo en guerras; no se oye otro que sitios, asaltos, batallas, degüellos, que hasta las mismas entrañas parece se han vuelto de bronce. . . .

mas yo digo que el de lodo cuando todo lo veo puesto dél; tanta inmundicia de costumbres, todo lo bueno por tierra; la virtud dió en el suelo con su letrero: "Aquí yace! . . ." al cabo al cabo, todo hombre es barro. (II, 701)

"In which century do you plan on living, in the one of gold or in the one of mire?"

"I would say," Critilo answered, "that it would be the one of iron. With so many errors, everything is amiss in the world and everything is backwards, if it is not already one of bronze, which is worse, with so many cannons and bombardments and everything burning in wars. You hear nothing else but sieges, assaults, battles, hangings, and it seems like even your soul has turned to bronze. . . ."

"[But] then I would say that the one of mire when I see everything turned into mire. So many unclean habits and everything good lying in it. Virtue fell to the ground with the sign 'Here I lie' . . . and in the end every man is made of clay."

Such are the wise man's cynical remarks concerning the times. Physicians are quacks and murderers, soldiers perpetuate wars, workers are lazy, lawyers and judges are incompetent, politicians are corrupt, preachers are pompous and affected, women are perfidious, and men are crazy.

National Psychology and Praise of Countries. Romera Navarro has pointed out Gracián's concern for the personalities of the nations that he satirizes: Germans are famous as gluttons and drunkards, Spaniards are proud, the French greedy, and the Portuguese boastful. The English are fickle and Protestant, the Italians are liars, and the Turks are barbarians. At the same time Gracián praises several countries, he simultaneously criticizes them. Spain, of course, is the most important nation in Europe, and she is both hated and envied. Italy is praised for her genius and her contributions to art, literature, philosophy, and political writings. Rome is the center of culture, history, religion and beautiful buildings. Lisbon is characterized as a good place with wealth, abundance, and a peculiar bent for the fantastic. France is "the flower of the kingdoms," blessed with holy kings and brave and wise men, while Brazil is a paradise of sugar.

Locus Amoenus. The topic of a beautiful, restful, and harmonious nature, a refuge *from* mankind, abounds in *The Master Critic,* especially in Crisis I and II of Part One.

Deus Artifex. God is the Maker of man as well as creator of a perfectly ordered universe, which is a perfect work of art:

Ese es—ponderó Critiilo—otro prodigioso efecto de la infinita sabiduría del Criador, con la cual dispuso todas las cosas en peso, con número y medida. Porque, si bien se nota, cualquiera cosa criada tiene su centro en orden al lugar, su duración en el tiempo y su fin especial en el obrar y en el ser. Por eso, verás que están subordinadas unas a otras, conforme al grado de su perfección. De los elementos que son los ínfimos en la naturaleza se componen los mixtos, y entre éstos los inferiores sirven a los superiores. Esas yerbas y esas plantas, que están en el más bajo grado de la vida, pues sola gozan la vegetativa, moviéndose y creciendo hasta un punto fijo de su perfección en el durar y crecer, sin poder pasar de allí, éstas sirven de alimento a los sensibles vivientes, que están en el segundo orden de la vida, gozando de la sensible sobre la vegetante, y son los animales de la tierra, los peces del mar, y las aves del aire. Ellos pacen la yerba, pueblan los árboles, comen sus frutos, anidan en sus ramas, se defienden entre sus troncos, se cubren con sus hojas y se amparan con su toldo. Pero unos y otros, árboles y animales, se reducen a servir a otro tercer grado de vivientes mucho más perfectos y superiores, que sobre el crecer y el sentir añaden el racionar, el discurrir y entender; y éste es el hombre, que finalmente se ordena y se dirige para Dios, conociéndole, amándole y sirviéndole. (I, 534—35)

This is the prodigious effect of the infinite wisdom of the Creator, whereby He organized all things in accordance with their weight, number, and measure: for, if one observes carefully [one sees that] every created thing has its center with respect to place, its duration in time, and its special end in action and existence. For this reason you will see that they are subordinated each to each in accordance with the degree of their perfection. The elements, which are lowest in the scale of nature, join to form mixed bodies; and among the latter, the lesser ones serve the greater. Those herbs and plants which are at the bottom of the scale of life (since their life is merely vegetative), moving and growing till they attain the point of their perfection with the passage of time beyond which point they cannot advance, nonetheless serve as nutriment for sentient beings, which are in the second rank of life, enjoying sentient life in addition to life which is merely vegetative; and these [sentient beings] are the animals of the earth, the fishes of the sea and the fowls of the air: these crop grass, live in trees whose fruit they eat, in whose branches they nest, among whose trunks they hide to defend themselves, with whose leaves they cover themselves, and beneath whose shade they take shelter from the sun. But all of them, trees and animals, live in the service of another and third rank of living beings, much more perfect and greatly superior, which, over and above growth and sense, can reason, ponder, and understand; and this is man, who at the end of the creative process is ordained and given existence for and toward God, to recognize Him, love Him, and serve Him.[12]

Arms and Letters. Gracián upholds the cerebral life of the Muses: music, literature, history, philosophy, political and spiritual writings. However, *The Master Critic* praises the life of the warrior who has fought (physically and/or figuratively) with the noble ends of honor and fame. Since heroism is a prime virtue for Gracián, the novel is indeed a catalogue of heroes both historical and fictional: Alexander the Great,, Vasco de Gama, Isabel and Ferdinand, James the Conqueror, The Cid, and so forth.

Fortune. This topic, which is a constant in all of Gracián's writings, is ambivalently portrayed as a capricious and powerful arbiter of life as well as a mediatress of justice and the divine world. She has favored Spain with "rivers of silver, mountains of gold, gulfs of pearls." The work speaks against her fickle nature and suggests that men neither blindly follow her nor humbly submit to her but rather face up to her with reason and good judgment.

Solitude. *The Master Critic* reflects upon this topic in both negative and positive ways. Critilo never restrains Andrenio's desire to be with the mad *vulgo*. On the one hand, solitude increases man's shortcomings, but on the other, solitude enables man to cultivate an interior life so that he can live wisely in a world of mediocrity and ordinary people.[12]

CHAPTER 5

Different Aspects of The Master Critic

I *Unifying Structural Elements*

NO doubt for many readers *The Master Critic* seems overwhelmingly fragmentary, a diffuse and intricate novel with highly disparate episodes and details. Yet, beyond the façade of what appears to be a loose narrative and little more than a catalogue of allegories and types, there exists a deliberate narrative design that is rich in technique and varied in literary devices. Gracián manages to bring together into one unifying context a vision of life based on imagination, moral philosophy, and experience. The finished product emerges as a coherent work, somewhat comparable to a baroque painting which, in its busy movement and multiple parts, finally projects a completeness and a totality. A discussion of the general structural features of *The Master Critic* and a close analysis of one of the *crisis* will provide insights into the artistic patterns of the work and identify the interrelated threads in the overall organization. One should see then that by no means is the work an assemblage of meaningless episodes and unconnected naration, but rather that the entire composition demonstrates that coherency functions within apparent incoherency, an aesthetic which indeed exemplifies baroque literary theory.

For centuries writers have used the pilgrimage or the journey to form the central narrative structure of their writings. It is precisely the journey of life developing in a temporal progression, a journey by the characters Andrenio and Critilo, that unifies the novel's thirty-eight *crisis* ("chapters of criticism"). Its three divisions archetypally recreate the three ages of man: Part One devotes thirteen chapters to Youth; Part Two, which also consists of thirteen chapters, traces the age of maturity; and Part Three, in twelve chapters, interprets Old Age. The reader is meant to be drawn into the series of these adventures, both as a participant and as an observer, for what he sees and what he reads is but a mirror of his own reality and destiny. Thus the reader is always conscious of these external forms of the journey within the framework of chronological time, as he is invited by an omniscient interpreter to continue the journey by reading the next chapter.

Furthermore, the work is governed by other general structural features. Its background is the world of human society, with Europe as an explicit geographic concept—a Europe of the Counter-Reformation with a consciousness of time past, present, and future. The protagonists pass through allegorical regions (City of Fools, World's Fair, Island of Immortality), mythical experiences (Salastano's magnificent library, the Learned Academy in Rome), and real and contemporary places (a both semireal and symbolic Madrid, Aragón, Italy, and so on). And whether these journeys take place in the earthly realm of life on the street, in the court, the palaces, the museums, and the like, or within imaginary realms that are inhabited by subhuman or inhuman creatures (the Cavern of Evils, the Dungeon of Death), what remains significant is that such extraordinary experiences lend another overall coherency to the *crisis*.

But most important, the key to the patterning of the work rests in allegory, the mode which serves as the primary unifying factor. Gracián himself attests to this in the preface of Part One, where he offers allegory as the synthesis of man's life and, by extension, his general plan of composition: "Judicious, unmalicious reader, I present to you today your life in a discourse." Romera Navarro[1] has studied the different dimensions of the vast range of allegories in *The Master Critic*. The following is his listing of these all-important allegorical "episodes" in the novel with added detail on narrative action and voice.

Part One

1. Debate Between Love and Fortune (iv); related by the author.
2. Humanity of the Beasts and Bestiality of Man (iv); Critilo is the speaker.
3. Uncivilized and Savage Childhood (v); description by the author while commentary is provided by the characters.

4. Crossroads of Life (v); Critilo and Andrenio are the actors of this allegory.

5. The Beastlike Citizens in the Main Plaza (vi); related from the point of view of the centaur Chiron.

6. Vices Fight for Preeminence in Dominating Man (vii); author's voice is heard.

7. Carriage of Deceit (vii); omniscient narrator.

8. Fountain of Deceits (vii); author's voice plus dialogue of the characters.

9. City of Deceit (vii); omniscient narrator with character participation and dialogue and with emphasis on thematic statement.

10. The Cheater on the Plaza of the Vulgar (vii); omniscient narrator in a playful tone. Critilo also delivers a diatribe against Machiavelli.

11. The Banquet of Deceits (vii); a combined narrative-dialogue structure in which the tone ranges from the burlesque to the very serious.

12. The Marvels of Artemia (viii); the crisi opens with the omniscient narrator as speaker. There are several references to historical figures.

13. Life is a Game (viii); the scene, a ballgame, is interpreted by an old man.

14. Falsimundo is Discovered (viii); highly descriptive with dialogues between Andrenio and the Prudent Man; they comment on the King of Deceit and his relatives.

15. Persecution of Wise Artemia by Deceit (ix); simple and brief. An omniscient narrator is in the background as Envy delivers a tirade against Artemia.

16. Artemia Flees the Court (x); a rather unimpressive allegory which turns out to be a descriptive catalogue of some Spanish cities.

17. The Universal Assault (x); technically and thematically excellent, with its satire and puns and its balance between dialogue and description.

18. Twins of Fortune (xi); a mixture of seriousness and mirth with an old man as narrator. The dialogue is interspersed with narration and a miscellany of historical allusions.

19. Falsirena's House (xii); brief, humorous allegory which centers around the House of Lust.

20. Egenio, Man With Six Senses (xii); satiric dialogues between Critilo and Egenio form part of the narrative action. There are many references to classical Greeks and Romans.

21. Cave of Lust (xii); a rapid and brief dialogue between the aforementioned characters, who describe the captives of Lust.

22. The Cavern of Evils (xiii); a recreation of Pandora's Box with Egenio as narrator.

23. The World's Fair (xiii); conversation among the characters. The event is characterized by a blend of comedy and social satire, with many allusions to historical and contemporary people.

Part Two

24. The Ages of Man (i); poetic allegory told by author.

25. Uphill Climb of Life (i); brief philosophic discussion between author, Critilo, and Andrenio.

26. Moral Argos (i); a lively dialogue with Argos as principal speaker.

27. Customhouse of Life (i); part of the narrative scheme with much action, dialogue, and social commentary regarding many eccentric types.

28. Dawn, Truth, and Friendship are not Welcome in the Palace (ii); story related by Argos.

29. The Best View in the Voyage of Life (ii); entirely in dialogue (Argos, Critilo, and Andrenio), with satiric and political commentary as well as a deprecation of modern times and praise of ancient times.

30. Quarrel of the French and Spanish Before Fortune (iii) opens the *crisi*. A burlesque satire against the French with a dialogue between Fortune and the French.

31. Moral Gerión (iii); dry, didactic allegory in dialogue which satirizes a few Spanish provinces.

32. Jail of Gold (iii); long, humorous allegory dominated by a dialogue which ridicules human passions and different character types.

33. The Palace of Wisdom (iv); omniscient narrator plus participation of several of the symbolic figures who speak to Critilo. Covers almost the entire chapter and literature and literary ideas are of importance.

34. Suitors of Happiness Entreat Fortune (v); a one-page allegory told by the author as a short satire against the courtiers.

35. The Plaza of the Vulgar Masses (v); popular language and humor abound in this long allegory, and dialogue predominates.

36. Man and Woman Ask for Favors Before the Divine Throne (vi); the *crisi* begins with, and is related to Critilo by, the Dwarf; it serves as a backdrop for the narrative action which ensues.

37. Fortune's Ladder (vi); Critilo is the principal speaker. Great use of antithesis and description.

38. Burdens and Discharges of Fortune (vi); a beautiful weaving together of illusion and reality through rapid dialogue.

39. Fortune's Table (vi); briefly narrated by the author. Proverbs and references to contemporary persons.

40. Fortune's Elder Daughter (vii) opens the *crisi*, linking chapters VI and VII to the extent that the previous action is continued.

41. Wasteland of Hipocrinda (vii); dialogue, vivid language, and satire fill this allegory, which constitutes almost an entire chapter.

42. Bravery's Last Will and Testament (viii); Bravery satirically narrates the story, which treats of national traits.

43. Bravery's Museum (viii); dialogue and many allusions to historical deeds and contemporary brave leaders.

44. The Man Who Waits for the Water of the River to Pass in Order to Cross It Without Getting Wet (ix); didactic allegory narrated by the author.

45. Amphitheater of Monstrosities (ix); crude and comical dialogue among several characters, especially those of the World, the Flesh, and the Devil.

46. Virtues are Forbidden (x); an omniscient narrator opens this chapter with another tale.

47. Virtelia is Found (x); a rather long allegory with a good balance between dialogue and narration. Much witty repartee and several popular sayings.

48. Vanity Seeks a Place Among Virtues (xi); a very brief allegory in the form of a debate between Vanity and Reason.

49. The Bridge of Buts (xi); a dramatic scene witnessed by the protagonists.

50. The Roof of Glass and Momo Throwing Stones (xi); dialogue and ingenious descriptions dominate the action.

51. Competition Between Arts and Science (xii); Shadow Man acts as narrator.

52. The Throne of Command (xii); political satire, dialogue, and Gracián's ever-constant pessimism dictate this section.

53. The Monster of Envy (xiii); almost entirely in dialogue form with particular emphasis on the unique characteristics of various provinces of Spain.

54. The Great Cage of Everyone (xiii); dialogue with humor, paradox, and puns. Critilo and Andrenio are observers.

Part Three

55. Honors and Horrors of Old Age (i—ii); perhaps the longest allegory, complete with dialogue, narration, action, and a gamut of moods.

56. The Dispensary of Vices (ii); anecdotes and dialogue. Mainly a condemnation of wine and drunkenness.

57. Dispute Among Physical and Spiritual Physicians (iii). The Correct Guesser relates the opening story to Critilo.

58. Truth in Childbirth (iii); puns, humor, and much slang characterize this allegory.

59. The Prestidigitator in the Great Plaza of the World (iv); the omniscient narrator is undermined by the characters whose scornful commentary, popular sayings, and comical remarks recreate the lively spectacle for the reader.

60. Deceit and Disillusion Take Each Other's Place on the

Threshold of Life (v); didactic allegory narrated by El Zahorí to the pilgrims.

61. The Palace Without Doors (v—vi); story alternates between the author's narration and Zahorí's; intercalated dialogue is also present.

62. Path of Astuteness and Path of Simplicity (vi); omniscient narrator as well as dialogue among the characters. A fable is interpolated.

63. The Court of Prudent Wisdom (vi); dialogue dominates and the allegory contains a series of allusions to the wise of all ages, an enumeration of buildings and figures as well as the Reform of Proverbs.

64. Battle Between Boastfulness and Laziness (vi); extensive dialogue as the travelers join in the battle.

65. Pride's Lofts (vii); strong censure of customs and traits (Spanish, French, and Portuguese); irony, dialogue, and humor prevail.

66. Meadows of Leisure (viii); same technique as previous allegory.

67. Cave of Nothingness (viii); narration and dialogue about literary criticism.

68. The Fool Who Searches for the Land of Contentment (ix); author is narrator.

69. The Wheel of Time (x); emphasis on the Spanish world. A blend of didacticism, criticism, and satire in the discussion of times past, present, and future.

70. Threads of Life (x); continuation of the former—similar in technique and theme.

71. Dancer on a Tight Rope (xi); brief allegory in dialogue form (Critilo, Andrenio, and the Courtier).

72. Inn of Life With Its Cave of Death (xi); description and animated dialogue between Death and her court. Humor and antithesis dominate.

73. Island of Immortality (xii); Critilo, Andrenio, and the Prodigious One engage in conversation. Some narrative description along with an artificial, stylized setting and numerous allusions.

Besides this pervasive use of allegory, the loosely threaded plot of thirty-eight *crisis* are held together by other interrelationships:

there is an interplay between allegorical reality and human reality; each *crisi*[2] generally begins with philosophic observation and ends in midaction; there is the tone of constant cynicism and scornful humor regarding man; Critilo and Andrenio and, of course, the author's controlling voice dominate throughout; the mythological types recur as basic features; moral and philosophic themes are the backbone of the narrative; complex style and difficult language provide rhetorical uniformity; the quest for Felisinda, happiness, and *desengaño* ("disillusionment") governs; comic spectacles and a series of events that represent the world and man in motion constitute a fundamental narrative base.

Another dimension of the overall structure of the work lies in the patterning of the first four chapters: these chapters form a microcosm of the total novel to the extent that they constitute a foreshadowing summary of themes, values, and philosophy and establish the basic relationship between Critilo and Andrenio. The whole of the novel, in a sense, is compressed into *Crisis* I—IV. In a quasi-biblical fashion, Gracián begins his story at the beginning of man, moves to antithetical discourse, and sets the stage within two narrative threads: Critilo and Andrenio. In the case of the former, the following motifs that will recur throughout the novel are introduced: shipwreck; the role of teacher and purveyor of knowledge; suffering in Goa; prison and anguish; liberation; near death at the hands of a greedy captain; betrayal by humanity; and the quest for Felisinda. Meanwhile, Andrenio's life has taken a different shape, as seen in the motifs relating to him: his early formation in a dark cave with beasts; isolation, and alienation; marvelous experiences and impressions as he contemplates exterior realities for the first time; comfort in the natural life; relative harmony with life; and quest for his mother. In these initial chapters, the two heroes converse at length about a medley of ideas, all central to the novel and recurring throughout it: variety; truth; beauty; nature; animals versus man; vices; passions; deprecation of man; and misanthropy; emphasis on *ser* ("being"), *parecer* ("appearing"); *ver* ("seeing"), and *saber* ("knowing"); art; and feminine cruelty to mention a few.

Perhaps a close analysis of the internal structure of one *crisi* will serve to bring Gracián's patterning of fictional reality into better focus. The casual reader will find that *Crisi* XI, Part Two, seems to represent yet another example of Gracián's lack of strict continuity in terms of characters or episodes. Nevertheless, the *crisi* is well written, and one can describe its anecdotal pattern as follows:

1. An interlude opens the chapter with a quasi-debate. Vanity defends herself as a virtue, while Reason rejects her as a brutal passion with no redeeming feature.

2. The Bridge of Buts over the River of Risibility is introduced. Several persons attempt to cross over to the Court of Honor, only to stumble on "buts" and "if it were not for that." Ridiculous types attempt to cross over, and the result is an interesting scene, peopled with jeering crowds. Among the characters are a famous but simple prince; an illustrious but rather uncharitable prelate; a famous but evil lawyer; a brave but dishonest soldier; a beautiful but stupid woman; a famous but unsuccessful doctor, and so on. Important ladies are sinfully adulterous, and the great lords turn out to be cowards.

3. There is a change of tempo in the Lesson of Life episode. A blind and mute man manages to cross the bridge by being sure not to trip on either his own or others' shortcomings; rather, he simply relies upon his own virtuous and significant works. Critilo and Andrenio also cross over by following the example of their blind peer.

4. In the palatial and magnificent City of Honor, the protagonists meet Momo, a little nothing of a man, who is symbolically a critical spirit and a destroyer of men's reputations. He is physically and spiritually repugnant: "He had a satyr's nose, stooped shoulders, an unbearable breath, which is a sign of worn out entrails . . ." (p. 797). Gossip is Momo's pastime, a specialization whereby he throws stones on glass roofs, leaving them all shattered; he also gleefully stains the inhabitants' faces with charcoal. The latter engage in banter and laughter with each other and do not know each other due to their masks of infamy and ignorance.

5. At the Practical Mirror, really the fountain at the plaza, these blighted souls blindly attempt, without success, to wash off the charcoal smudges of their moral and spiritual deficiencies. The water and its reflections only serve to emphasize these weaknesses and shortcomings.

6. Next comes the search for honor wherein several types of men try to find a worldly, false brand of honor and mistakenly identify

honor with wealth, power, lineage, or the avenging of an affront.

7. It is difficult to find honor in present times. The solution is that honor is found in death. Honor did exist in times past when great men lived.

8. There follows a delightful description of the wise and widely feared governor *Qué Dirán* ("What will they say"), who represents the conscience and keeper of honor in former times. People from all strata were his subjects: princes, professors, heroes, judges, women, widows, soldiers, wise men.

9. *Qué Dirán* is defeated and dismissed by the masses of vulgar, common people. Honor is declared nonexistent.

10. Momo's opposite, Mr. Yes-Yes or Bobo ("Fool"), symbol of flattery and acquiescence, appears on the scene. His names number many, while his world remains a simple, pleasant place.

11. An impending battle ensues between the forces of Momo, composed of such followers as the critics, the crafty, the satirists, and the defamers, who are pitted against Bobo's forces of dolts, weak men, and agreeable simpletons. The narrative is suspended in midaction.

12. Critilo and Andrenio are invited to go off in search of Honor, and the reader is issued a parallel invitation to go on to the next *crisi* to find out what happens.

The chapter, although possessing a zigzag scheme, does move from one motif or episode to the next quite easily and naturally. What lends internal unity besides this anecdotal chain of events, which in this case focus primarily on honor, are the vibrant tones of the language throughout the *crisi* and the gallery of voices. Gracián even uses some Italian as he stresses the absurdity of Momo's counterpart, Bobo, in describing his name as *manjia con tuti* [sic] ("he who eats with everyone") and *bono bono* ("Mr. Yes-Yes"). Reality is then conveyed through the different perspectives of the various types along with an omniscient author who stays behind the scenes to judge, praise, or condemn the actions and issues of the moment.

From the point of view of language, Gracián successfully captures the tones, styles, and forms of speech that best reflect the nature of each character. Both Vanity and Reason speak in cerebral and rather cold terms as they discuss the question of virtue at the start of the chapter. At the Bridge of Buts, when the author intercepts the action, he speaks in a very scornful, sarcastic manner as he censures man's follies, although, of course, his statements are more abstract and more complicated. Then there is the jeering crowd who make comments. Their statements are generally simple stylistically and conceptually. One finds, for instance, a remark such as "Oh, how delicate is a face since the slightest blemish shows" (p. 796).

Critilo, on the other hand, appears as an objective judge of human behavior. His voice, as Gracián's alter ego, is temperate, yet often satirical, as in the case when he addresses himself to the characters and the reader alike saying: "This blind man must be our guide since only the blind, the deaf, and the silent can now live in the world. Let us learn this lesson; let us be blind to the shortcomings of others, silent so as not to criticize them nor overvalue ourselves, reconciling hatred with gossip in reciprocal vengeance" (p. 796).

By contrast, we find a group of characters who engage in a game of blemish; their jargon is rapid, playful, and exclamatory:

"Don't you see what an awful stain so and so has in his lineage? And that he dare to speak about others!"
"For he cannot see that his own infamy is so notorious and starts talking about others! No one has honor on his tongue!"
"Look who's talking . . . having the wife he has! How much better it would be were he to look after his own house and know where this flashy woman comes from."
"For he is unable to see that he has good reason to be quiet, having such a sister that we all know about!"
"How much better would it be that he remember his grandfather and who he was! That's the way it is, the ones who talk the most should talk the least!"

Then Momo himself becomes an extension of the Critilo-Gracián combination. His voice is the same as theirs—strong, serious, and critical—and his intent is the same: to teach mankind to be aware through *seeing* and *knowing*. His discussions refer to many of the same themes: women, ancient versus modern times, man's stupidity, the problem of honor, and the widespread sense of inferiority, both social and intellectual. Interestingly enough, the voice of Bobo cannot be heard directly; instead, the reader acquires only a bare knowledge of him through the voices of Momo and Andrenio.

Another unifying feature is Gracián's preoccupation with *culture* throughout the chapter (and the work), a culture that he records in his use of popular sayings; proverbs; allegories; and a vast range of allusions to people, places, and events; and to the mythological guide, Momo, who in ancient times was the god of ridicule and a literary creation of Lucian. Gracián is concerned not only with the culture of Spain but also with culture in a universal sense. Even the language that he employs gives insight into culture. It is with amazing facility that the characters and the omniscient narrator engage in verbal games and are able to turn a phrase quickly or to glibly flavor a comment with a pun.

Finally, one sees a consistency in Gracián's penchant for summarization in his narrative art. Just as the first four chapters of the novel serve as a summary of the entire work, so does the very last part of *Crisi* XII, Part Three function as a summary. To tie up the disparate uses of allegory, Gracián neatly reviews the trajectory of allegories and virtues as well as all the experiences of the protagonists that won them the right to enter the Island of Immortality. The omniscient narrator concludes the novel with the following recapitulatory remarks:

And at that moment the Pilgrim came up and begged for him and his two comrades to be allowed to enter. Merit asked for their certificate and asked if it was legalized by Bravery and authenticated by Fame. He began to examine it very purposefully and began to raise his eyebrows with signs of astonishment. And when he saw it distinguished with so many titles from Philosophy in the great Theater of the Universe, from Reason and her lights in the Valley of Beasts, from Attention at the Entrance of the World, from Self-Knowledge in the Moral Evaluation of Man, from Completeness in the False Step of Surprise, from Circumspection at the Fountain of Deceits, from Awareness in the Courtly Gulf, from Warning in Falsirena's house, from Sagacity at the General Fair, from Prudence at the Universal Reform, from Curiosity in Salastano's house, from Generosity in the Jail of Gold, from Knowledge in the Museum of the Discreet, from Uniqueness in the Plaza of the Masses, from Happiness at the Steps of Fortune, from Soundness in the Convent of Hipocrinda, from Bravery in his Armory, from Virtue in her Enchanted Palace, from Fame among the Rooftops of Glass, from Mastery at the Throne of Command, from Judgment in the Cage of

Everyone, from Authority among the Horrors and Honors of Old Age, from Moderation in the Dispensary of Vices, from Truth giving birth, from Disillusion in the World Deciphered, from Caution in the Palace Without Doors, from Knowledge reigning, from Humility in the House of the Fatherless Daughters, from Great Worthiness in the Cave of Nothingness, from Happiness discovered, from Constancy at the Wheel of Time, from Life in Death, from Fame on the Island of Immortality, he opened wide the Arch of Triumph to the Mansion of Eternity.

What they saw there were the things they had achieved—he would know them and experience them, [and he would] let him take the path of matchless Virtue, of Heroic Bravery, and he will end up at the Theater of Fame, at the Throne of Esteem and at the Center of Immortality. (III, 1010—11)

II   The Master Critic and *Gracián's Theory of Literary Criticism.*

Gracián is acknowledged to have written the major literary treatise of the Spanish seventeenth century as well as one of the outstanding works of fiction. Therefore, it would be advantageous to see how he used some of his well-defined literary concepts in his own creative writing. *The Master Critic,* then, in addition to being a compendium of Gracián's moral philosophy as found in his earlier treatises like *The Hero, The Discreet Man,* and *The Art of Worldly Wisdom* also represents a praticum for the literary precepts found in his *The Mind's Wit and Art.* Of course, one would expect to find such an interrelationship between Gracián the literary theoretician of baroque aesthetics and Gracián the artist of unmistakable brilliance and density.

Much has been written concerning the possible sources of *The Master Critic*—Gracián openly identifies many of them—and comparisons have been made, for example, with Cervante's *Quijote* and *Persiles and Sigismunda,* with Barclay's *Satyricon,* and with Boccalini's *Ragguagli.* But in spite of the many influences, the work does emerge as an original and complex novel. Its originality lies precisely in that mode of wit expounded in *The Mind's Wit and Art*—a wit that provides delight and moral truths about man's conduct and is bound to the Horatian *utile et dulce.* As a work of art, Gracián's fiction appeals to the intellecutal and the curious, to those who search for a medley of emotions and moods combined with cerebral impact. Consequently, *The Master Critic* carries out one of Gracián's major literary precepts, that of originality. True, he debunks the idea that originality in the purist, radical sense really exists. But what he does suggest is an originality which broadens man's perspective concerning himself and the universe around him, an originality which emphasizes the rare, the unique, and the astounding. Perhaps this is an excessive burden for the artist; yet Gracián adheres to his interpretation of originality, a blend of many elements that permit one to characterize *The Master Critic* as a novel of exceptional inventiveness. Particularly original are the strong ideas regarding moral philosophy; Gracián's skillful and violent distortions of reality through the grotesque descriptions of man disguised as a monster or disguised with carnival masks;[3] the frequent use of puppet and marionette images to convey man's psychological deterioration and dehumanization; a narrative which moves the reader abruptly from the realm of reality to the realm of fantasy; the accumulation of allegories that break away from classical restraints and move toward wild deformation and exaggeration; a Quevedo-like and mordant satire on individuals taken from all walks of life and on collective society as well; a collage of commentary concerning the social order—or rather social disorder—and customs; mythological monsters and characters of his own creation such as the Shadow Man and "Dwarf-Giant"; a gamut of narrative tones which ranges over an apparent spontaneity, frenzy, silence, pessimism, tragicomedy, and so on.

Overwhelming heed is paid the precept of erudition in *The Mind's Wit and Art:* a work of value must be complex, learned, and replete with recondite images and intricate comparisons and metaphors. The reader of *The Master Critic* must labor to attain knowledge and to capture the many scholarly allusions; correspondences with ancient literatures, allegories, and history; and the extensive references to people and places of all times. The very erudite Critilo, of course, acts as a *magister:* indeed, a relationship between erudition and life is fundamental to the work. Furthermore, besides being a literary precept, erudition is a moral and ethical virtue, not merely gentlemanly polish.

Of primary concern in the aesthetics of *The Mind's Wit* is the creation of a literature of beauty based on variety, antithesis, and tension. Gracián shapes the entire narrative structure of his novel in terms of antithesis, beginning with the contrasting nature of the major characters themselves. In fact, the entire work rest on duality and on a multiplicity of reality as well as on a series of contrasting manners in the perception of reality. Critilo and Andrenio depict "opposites" regarding their world view, social behavior, personality traits, and complementary perceptions of reality. The novel involves a constant play of antithetical contrasts: *engaño* vs. *desengaño* ("deception vs. disillusionment"); *ser* vs. *parecer* ("being vs. seeming"); the visible perception of reality vs. the intuitive, the abstract, thought, and imagination; the obvious vs. the obscure; prudence vs. foolishness; wonder vs. confrontation; the exterior physical world vs. the interior mental world; good judgment vs. pleasure. In varying degrees the novel portrays—or rather elaborates, defines, and redefines—these paradoxical issues which convey the Golden Age's positive attitude (so central to the aesthetics of *The Mind's Wit)* toward the juxtaposition of opposites and the supreme value of exposing man to, and reminding him of, the interplay of contrasts and counterpoint in the universe.

Gracián explores many ideas regarding the literary experience and the nature of literature. As a theoretician, he addresses himself to the literary from of the *crisi* in Discourses 27 and 38 of *The Mind's Wit.* Interestingly enough, *The Master Critic* is composed of thirty-eight chapters called *crisi*, which are, in essence, critiques or ponderations about man and life. Since there is a loose narrative thread with neither a psychological nor a mythic continuity, each *crisi* can be read as an autonomous chapter to the extent that each embraces some aspect of life and a corresponding moral truth. The literary doctrine of Gracián hails the *crisi* as an appropriate means for censure, ingenuity, and clever satire, elements all concomitant with *The Master Critic.*

In Discourse 55 of *The Mind's Wit,*[4] the art of allegory and parables is discussed:

The ordinary method of disguising the truth in order the better to insinuate it without strife is that of parables and allegories. They should not be long, nor in a continued series; one of them from time to time will refresh the taste and turn out quite well. If it is didactic it ought to aim for disillusionment toward the sublime, and will then be well received. (p. 807)

But in the novel we find that Gracián deviates from his own dictum simply because he accumulates scores of allegories (a time-honored literary tradition in all literatures for conveying moral philosophy) and allows his pen to fly into fantasy within the framework of a wide variety of allegories. In fact, in the preface, he advises the reader of his intent to present an allegory of man's life. Romera-Navarro has pointed out the panoramic scope of the allegories in *The Master Critic*, which range from the serious, dramatic, and satirical to the humorous, intellectual, practical and, poetic.[5] Although the allegories are intercalated throughout the entire work, the general format is that each *crisi* is introduced by an allegory, apologue, or fable told by a character (sometimes Critilo) or the author himself; Critilo and Andrenio then experience in some way the lesson which the story elaborates. And it is by means of allegory that Gracián is able to combine the pleasures of the imagination, philosophy, and social criticism, as prescribed by *The Mind's Wit*.

Popular philsophy via maxims and proverbs also figures in *The Master Critic*. In Discourse 43 of *The Mind's Wit* maxims are discussed as a powerful "genre" for truth, perception, education and wit. We might mention here that the Jesuit again deviates from his standard critical demand for an aristocratic literature by espousing this form of popular expression, for indeed, he liberally sprinkles common proverbs throughout all of his writing. It is the proverb or the maxim that provides him with one more means to moralize. Besides the delightful "Reform of Proverbs" of *Crisi* VI, Part Three, we find a medley of sayings which endorse a commonsense approach to life:

"Make yourself famous and then rest on your laurels."
"All that glitters is not gold."
"In the land of fools, the madman is king."
"Man is not king of the world but the slave of woman."
"The first step in ignorance is presumption."

Fiction, says Gracián, is used by those "serious" authors who endeavor to teach important political and moral doctrines. Two aspects of fiction, metamorphosis and the narration of "the marvelous," are discussed in his literary theory and likewise adhered to in his narrative art. Concerning metamorphosis, he asserts that it is an extraordinary literary technique which bridges the natural and moral world, thereby providing wisdom and artistic pleasure. In the same vein he writes:

To the extraordinariness of metamorphosis may be added the entertainment of the narration of the marvelous, in which the difficulty lies in knowing how to construct the entanglement and the intertwining stringencies and pressures; and the more complicated they become, the more delightful they make the design and artifice. (p. 814)

A detailed examination would reveal how extensively both modes are developed in *The Master Critic.* For example, in general terms, we witness the metamorphosis of Critilo and Andrenio, especially the latter in the physical, spiritual, and mental sense as he progresses through the labyrinth of life. More specifically, there are many passages which underline changes undergone by the characters, as in this vivid description:

for women never want to grow old; they always want to be young girls. See how lame Time has furrowed the foreheads of some, and dragging them by their hair, he has plucked off the best ornament of nature. See what a blow he has given to one by allowing her teeth to drop out and her eyebrows to rot with years. How he has transformed their beauty into an uncomely mask. (I, 565)

We are transported into the aura of all that is "marvelous" as we share the happenings. The "marvelous" in *The Master Critic* consists of such elements as the touchstone, which examines Good and Evil for the travelers; the Wheel of Time, which scans all facets of time; the Cave of Nothingness; the prodigious miracles of Artemia, who gives life to statues, creates angels from monsters and human beings from lions, and makes the stupid very smart—and these are only a few of her magical feats mentioned by Gracián.

It is not surprising to learn that the Jesuit was keenly conscious in theory and practice of the visual effect of literature; he mentions Hieronymus Bosch and the *capricho* in Crisi VI, Part One. And, as one follows the journey of the protagonists, some of Bosch's allegorical art comes to mind: "The Garden of Eden," which depicts the tortures of the damned in hell and purgatory, along with the animals that symbolize vices which lead to man's downfall; "The Hain Wain," which presents the dangers encountered by the travelers on the road of life and their episodes with Good and Evil; the famous "Garden of Delights," which portrays the sensual pleasures. Gracián paints these same scenes with words in *The*

Master Critic. Furthermore, in Discourse 57 of his literary treatise, he speaks about the emblem, a symbolical picture with words usually on a moral subject, as a "sublime genre" and "the motto is the soul of the picture; it must include wit." He refers to the emblems of Andrea Alciato in both *The Mind's Wit* and *The Master Critic*.[6] Most interesting is his personal application of emblematic techniques in his writing to paint pictures with words, pictures that challenge the eye and mind of the reader as well as heighten the elusive nature of a constantly changing and shifting reality (the pictorial emblem, of course, was customarily accompanied by a prose explanation). Thus, his graphics of words are read and imagined, not seen like the actual emblems. His pictures turn out to involve swans, water-mirror images, the dove-serpent image or images of beautiful nature, incisive portraits of human squalor and repulsive situations, along with skillfully drawn descriptions of monsters, centaurs, satyrs, serpent men, and the like.

A further aesthetic point of departure for Gracián centers on style and language, on subtlety in form and content. In his novelistic art, he is a masterful practitioner of what he preaches regarding stylistic versatility, syntax, and vocabulary—an excessive style which piles words upon words and phrases upon phrases so as to exploit the great expressive potential of language. His love of words with multiple and equivocal meanings is most evident in his constant and almost tiresome use of puns. In *The Master Critic* the pun is the device which serves as a vehicle for humor and ridicule, and as the means of stressing serious thoughts. As a theoretician, Gracián views the rhetorical device as a source of wit and ingenuity and as an artist he utilizes its various modes: double entendre, homonyms, paronomasia and syllepsis. Puns are for him an instrument for commenting on the human comedy—personality quirks, physical characteristics, personal habits, moral formation, false values, national traits. Punning is Gracián's favored device of ridicule, satire, and disparagement, the ingredients of the all-pervading tone of the novel.

The Mind's Wit does not address itself to the problem of a nominal style per se, but it does discuss verbal style. If one were to classify the style of *The Master Critic*, he would have to describe it as equally verbal and nominal in that the prose is heavily charged with both forms. Gracián says of verbs that "the nerve of style consists in the intensive profundity of the verb. There are those that are significant, full of soul, that express things with doubled emphasis; a seasoned selection of them makes language perfect" (p. 865). And perhaps adhering to the tradition of the Latinate style, Gracián extensively avails himself of the preterite tense. In fact, he relegates most action to the distant past, even those events that have just occurred. In this preponderance of verbs, however, the reader discovers the frequent use of bimembration and polymembration, figures which not only intensify movement but also reinforce the interplay of contrasts, a major thematic feature of the entire composition, to be sure:

Antithetical Bimembration	"Nature was a stepmother to man, for what she took from him at birth she gives back to him at death" (p. 520).
Accumulative Polymembration	"for besides those five very vigorous senses, he [Egenio] had another sense which was better than all the others and which stimulates the rest and causes us to reason and to find things no matter how hidden they may be; it contrives, finds ways, provides remedies, teaches speaking, makes us run and even fly and divines the future: this sense is Necessity" (pp. 640–41).

The bimembration and polymembration of nouns function with the same intensity and with the same emphasis on antithesis:

"Litotic" Bimembration	"There is a great difference between immortal fame and eternal infamy" (p. 1010).
Hyberbolic Polymembration	"So sweet conversation is the banquet of understanding, food for the soul, relief for the heart, attainment of knowledge, life of friendship and the best activity of man" (p. 997).

Gracián is famous for combining adverbs and adjectives such as "fácilmente dificultoso" ("easily difficult") or "valorosamente religioso" ("bravely religious").[7] His style also includes the use of two adjectives in apposition with no conjunction (asyndeton): "soberana callada majestad" ("sovereign silent majesty"), "aquella infinita increada belleza" ("that infinite uncreated beauty"), as well as compound nouns: "universo espejo" ("universe-mirror").

Although Gracián theoretically argues for an "eclectic style," that is, the middle road of the "natural style" somewhere between the Asiatic and Laconic style, he departs from his treatise by employing a dominantly hyperbolic and conceitful baroque mode of expression in *The Master Critic*, a style that, with its unrestrained long sentences, distinctive idioms, unusual series of images, and dramatic situations and tensions, is syntactically difficult. Many other parallels between the Jesuit's literary precepts and his own literary practice can also be evaluated such as questions relating to his theory of wit and conceitful writing, like hyberbole, heroic events, epithets, overstatements, enigmas, allusions, and quick replies, all treated in *The Mind's Wit*. But one thing is certain: Gracián strikes a balance in fitting together his analytic aesthetic views and his artistic experience as a creative writer, as evidenced by the correspondences between his literary doctrine and his novel.

III *Life and Literary Theory in* The Master Critic

One of the most prominent characteristics of *The Master Critic* is the way in which Gracián relates his concepts of literature to his outlook on life. Ideas concerning literature are scattered throughout the three books of the novel, and it would be difficult to see in them any pattern other than one which emerges from their relationship to Gracián's commentary on man. The following discussion will show how Gracián relates letters to life.

A relationship between life, literature, and art is constantly stressed throughout Gracián's work of fiction. Critilo and Andrenio represent for Gracián a dual aspect of life: the elevated and the ordinary. The imaginative arts, however, address themselves only to the aristocratic and educated man, and all facets of art provide the latter with a means of cultivating the spirit and the intellect. This idea seems to reflect Aristotle's idea that philosophy, although apparently useless and impractical, is most necessary for man. Gracián transfers Aristotle's opinion on philosophy to art in his references to art as a refinement of reality, for art and literature give harmony to man's orderless world. For example, he writes that "where artifice does not mediate, all nature becomes distorted" (I, 522).

In the vast arena of life in which Gracián's characters struggle, artistic beauty is never substituted for morality. Rather, *The Master Critic* finds that art, like morality, is a means for moral behavior. The secrets and mysteries of life are many and one way to reach an understanding of life is through instructive reading. Books are food for the soul and delight for the spirit, as well as a means of reaching Gracián's guiding ideal of "being a person" and "being a man." Finding himself in Salastano's [i.e., Lastanosa's] library,[8] Critilo exclaims:

> There is no flattery, there is no advantage for someone who is ingenious like a new book every day. . . . Oh, what pleasure reading, the employment of persons who, if reading can't find them, create them! (II, 709)

Since time is an integral part of life, the protagonists discuss its causes and effects. The effect of time on literature is pondered, and in this regard, Critilo reflects Gracián's rare optimism about artistic expression: the best is yet to be said in life, letters, and art. And with reference to the cyclical nature of art and literature, Critilo points out that great periods of productivity are followed by decline and sterility in the creative arts. Gracián extends this idea to the life span of man: for there is nothing that is stable, and everything is climb and ascent" (III, 966).

In *The Master Critic* literature and art are further linked to life through the world of imagination: the imaginative arts allow man to experience in his own life the world that he finds in letters. Thus, Critilo judges harshly those works which have nothing to say or teach. He supports the didactic precepts of *The Mind's Wit* and insists that art and literature instruct as well as delight the audience. Moreover, Critilo supports Gracián's idea that there is no substitute for life; not even the imagination is able to grasp all the subtleties of life, and thus art is designated as inferior to life by the Decipherer:

> You will be men by dealing with those that are, for that is just what seeing the world means. Because note that there is a great difference between seeing and looking, for he who does not understand, does not

notice: it is of little importance to see a lot with the eyes if there is no understanding, nor is there any value in seeing without taking note. He was so right who said that the best book in the world is the world itself. (III, 877)

And when Envy delivers her tirade, Gracián perceives a flaw in artistic creation to the extent that it detracts from real life:

"Note that after this make-believe queen has introduced herself into the world, there is no truth, everything is adulterated and feigned, nothing is what it seems to be, for her procedure is for half the year to be with art and deceit and the other half deceit and art." (I, 607)

Critilo also explains to an as yet unsophisticated Andrenio that art gives the ugly and the ordinary aspect of life the illusion of beauty. Art and literature ennoble nature and constitute a source of truth; therefore, the imaginative arts intensify man's life by elevating his spirit and by freeing him from an ugly and monotonous world. As the two pilgrims experience life in their allegorical journey, they often see in the world an imitation of reality. They recognize that man has a natural tendency and instinct to imitate—even Andrenio seeks to imitate his teacher, Critilo. Echoing the Platonic concept of imitation, one of Critilo's guides states that the world is an imitation of an imitation.[9] This idea of life may also be applied to the concepts of literature and art: "Believe me that everything artificial is but a shadow in terms of the natural, and nothing but a poor imitation" (III, 854).

The Master Critic affirms not only that literature and art offer insights into life, but also that man is transported into a historical moment or literary moment by means of the writer's or artist's ingenuity. This particular posture is most evident in the meeting in Salastano's library, where the various figures recount the merits of particular literary or historical contributions. And when Andrenio finally reaches maturity, he is able to relate artistic creation to the exterior and interior nature of life. The painter interprets for us the exterior reality of the world while the writer gives verbal expression to the inner reality of life: "for we see that the painter's brush only portrays the exterior but the pen, the interior, and the advantage of one over the other is that of the body over the soul" (III, 917).

The themes of the ugliness and uncertainty of life underlie the novel, reflecting the baroque aesthetic of ugliness and surprise in art. Critilo's statement reveals his comprehension of the baroque artistic currents and the effects produced upon the beholder: " 'You have seen up until now the works of nature and admired them with good reason. You will see from now on the works of artifice, which should frighten you' " (I, 551).

The travels of life, in *The Master Critic*, turn out to be arduous, sometimes grotesque, often tumultuous. Likewise, the difficulty of life matches the difficulty of artistic expression. No creative work of eminence reaches The Island of Immortality unless it is the result of a long and hard labor: " 'for as much as one sweats and works, so much also will be his fame and immortality' " (I, 652—53). And this problem of artistic creation is further complicated by the fact that originality is almost impossible: " 'There you will see that things are the same as they were; only memory is lacking. Nothing happens that has not been, nothing that can be called new under the sun' " (III, 965).

Then at the Island of Immortality, the protagonists are impressed by the *chalupa de arte* ("the raft of art") which represents many facets of life. The tools that are necessary for art and literature are also necessary for a successful life—wisdom, ingeniousness, and moral purpose:

He then chartered a canoe made of the sturdiest cedar and inlaid with ingenious inscriptions like gold and vermilion illuminations with a relief of emblems and figures taken from Jovio, Saavedra, Alciato and Solórzano. (III, 996)

The relationship between life and the imaginative arts can therefore be said to be a general thread that runs through the novel. On a more specific level, poetry signifies "que para el gusto no hay cosa como la Poesía" ("for taste, there is nothing like poetry"). A poet makes this comment to the two travelers at one point, and one understands that poetry is viewed as profit and enjoyment. But profit has an intellectual and moral meaning, an idea which is in full accord with Gracián's poetic theory in *The Mind's Wit*.

But since beauty and pleasure are closely tied to poetry, Gracián reflects upon still another position: poets are not to be taken too seriously, for their life and their art, too, are subject to rules. On the other hand, through Critilo's voice, the reader is given an insight into the nature of a poem; a poem viewed as "creation" rather than "imitation":[10] " 'As far as I am concerned,' said Critilo, 'Horace lost them [poetic instruments] when he most wanted to win them, discouraging them with his rigorous precepts' " (II, 715).

In the same vein, Critilo is always urging his pupil and companion to approach life with originality, perspective, and spontaneity. The poem is to be an expression of the foregoing qualities of life as well as a permanent communication joined with the element of *admiratio*. What is significant in *The Master Critic* is that poetry deals with life, with the world, and with history. The almost perfect combination of the moral and the fictitious is to be found in the epic, while yet another attribute of poetry is the poem as panegyric

True poety is intellectual and spiritual in nature; that is a position found in *The Mind's Wit* and developed in *The Master Critic*. The popular poetry of the ballads, which is the poetic expression of the masses, is severely criticized and condemned. Critilo is witness to this judgment in his adventure in the key episode concerning the *Reforma de Libros* ("Book Reform"):

> . . . and generally every kind of poetry in a vulgar language [i.e., a non-Latin one], especially burlesque and amorous poetry, *letrillas* [a form of occasional poetry], comic ballads, interludes, spring foliage [all], were handed over to the fops. (II, 675)

That intellectual and abstract poetry should veil knowledge and pleasure from the crude masses reaffirms Gracián's division of life into an intellectual aristocracy and an unthinking populace. Moreover, in his novel, Gracián would have us seek in the poem the same kind of challenge that life presents to man. That is, a poem that uses the most contrary metaphors is the most delightful because "todo es hazer y padecer" ("everything is doing and suffering") and the universe is filled with contrasts. What happens in life must happen in the poem. The difficulty of life for man is reflected in the difficulty of comprehension, which is characteristic of the poem. One age stresses the moral importance of poetry; another, the formal beauty. The aesthetics of *The Master Critic* as related by different characters, especially Critilo, propose both moral and formal beauty in poetry.

In summary, then, the relationship between *The Master Critic* and life can be described as follows: the novel has a double point of reference, and Gracián engages in a tandem judgment on life and literature, which he sees as inextricably entwined. The general nature of *The Master Critic* lies in the use of a philosophic-didactic artifice that aspires to universal moral and aesthetic values: *The Master Critic* is the most outstanding work of seventeenth-century Spanish literature to effect a presentation of literary ideas through fiction, and Gracián has sought to express what he believes to be true of life. Finally, he considers literature, like life, in the broadest and most sweeping of critical terms. In the final analysis, for both art as well as man's life, Gracián is insistently the most demanding and authoritative "Master Critic."

CHAPTER 6

The Complete Man: Gracián's Treatises on Human Values

I The Hero

IN all literary traditions writers have sought to formulate a definition of man. As a consequence, the theme of heroism has opened a fruitful realm of possibilites for this inquiry, particularly in the case of that heroism that is concomitant with wisdom and with physical and spiritual courage. The topic of heroism, this aggrandizement and lordliness of man as well as the quest for the essence of extraordinary human beings, has been a constant intellectual and literary challenge. Spanish writers of the seventeenth century were especially drawn to the concept of heroism, for example, Quevedo, Saavedra Fajardo, and Juan Henríquez Zúñiga.

Gracián's *El héroe* (The Hero) may be placed within the framework of the ethicopolitical writings of the Spanish baroque. But in a far broader context, the treatise shares with all writers who sought to shape man's values the expression of the heroic ideals which govern a distinguished and exceptional life. Of course, Gracián was influenced by writers before him: Pliny the Younger (*Panegyric to Trajan*), Castiglione (*The Courtier*), Machiavelli (*The Prince*),[1] Juan Rufo (*Las seiscientas apotegmas* [Six Hundred Short Sayings]), and Botero (*Detti memorabili di personaggi* [Memorable Sayings of Persons]). More significant is the far-reaching influence of *The Hero* through its various translations into French, English, and Italian, and its impact upon men such as Nuño Alvares Pereda in Portugal, Ceriziers and Corneille in France, and Schopenhauer and Nietzsche in Germany.

The Hero, published defiantly in 1637 without approval by his

Jesuit superiors and under the pen name of Lorenzo Gracián, Infanzón, represents Gracián's first literary endeavor. It is a very short treatise of twenty *primores* ("excellencies"), which were written for a very select few, like Philip IV, to whom he dedicated his autographed manuscript. The 1637 first edition was dedicated to his friend Juan Lastanosa, and the second honored Juan Bautista Brescia but was signed by Pedro de Quesada. The three dedications are interrelated by the common theme—that of the miniature size of the book.

Highly conscious of his purpose in this first attempt at writing, Gracián states that his aim was to speak to leaders and to great men, to aspirants to heroism. In the prologue to the reader he says:

How exceptional do I wish you to be! I undertake to shape a giant man with a midget book and produce a maximum man with brief periods [sentences] and immortal deeds. This is a miracle in perfection.[2]

His ideas, as he sees it, present "un espejo manual," "the book as a mirror," *topos* in which man can recognize himself as he is and as he should be. Gracián also clarifies his other objectives: to offer a means to distinction presented in a few rules via a terse style.

After this introductory commentary, Gracián directly imparts his tidy plan for greatness by writing twenty prescriptions for it, that is, for being a Catholic hero in life. Perhaps the lofty ideals he sets forth may not really be within the reach of mortals, but his total plan of principles presents some interesting challenges. His contact with the reader in the first treatise is a bit distant; there exists the aloofness that allows for some apparently deliberate patronizing familiarity (he uses the familiar *tú* ["thou"] form, although this may be more an imitation of the neutral Latin pronoun). His voice is full of authority and superiority as he effects distancing through his favorite technique of willful obscurity and the use of some indefinable terminology such as *destreza* (skill, agility) and *despejo* (elusiveness or *je ne sais quoi*). Monroe Z. Hafter addresses himself to the problem of Gracián's loftiness of manner, which is attentuated in his later works.[3]

Rhetorical eulogy and an epithetical style with an abundant use of antithesis, anecdotes, and digressions describe the general features of the treatise. In the role of the preacher-advisor, Gracián alludes to former times and famous people—again his penchant for history and its distinguished personages is apparent—and his models of excellence and persons to be imitated include such figures as Ferdinand, Isabella, Alexander the Great, Caesar, Louis XII of France, Solomon, and Charles V—a panorama of individuals who are to march across the pages of his subsequent works. As advisor, Gracián equips the potential hero with the wherewithal to cope with man and society in order to attain the state of perfection as a Catholic hero. His negative attitude toward the *vulgo*, the masses, as well as his fundamental cynicism pervade this work and all the others to follow.[4]

One notes that Gracián's set of premises in the formation of his abstract protagonist, the hero, are eclectic in nature, but then one finds that eclecticism, moral as well as literary, is a constant in Gracián's writings. Thus, his aspirant to perfection in this world must possess a multiplicity of talents and excellent qualities. Indeed, he emerges as a mixture of a superman, a quasi-divine individual, a skillful leader, and an astute politician, a prudent and wise man, a creative artist, an accomplished warrior, an outstanding ruler, and a distinguished gentleman. The true Catholic hero must be able to transcend difficulties and society; he must dissemble, emulate, and transcend as well as have the capacity to see beyond superficial circumstances and reality. Throughout the treatise, Gracián refers to the hero as *varón culto* ("learned man"), *varón excelente* ("excellent man"), *varón prudente* ("prudent man"), *varón máximo* ("great man"), *varón eminente* ("eminent man"), and *varón raro* ("unique man").

However, such powers and perfections are secondary to the perfection discussed in Primor XX; it is the absolute perfection, virtue. The Jesuit ends his composition on a Thomistic, thoroughly Catholic note:

Greatness cannot be found in sin, which is nothingness, but in God who is everything. To be a hero of the world means nothing or little; to be a hero of Heaven means a great deal, whose great King would be praised, honored and glorified.

And although the hero must possess this virtue and spirituality, Gracián devotes his attention in his essay to pragmatic values and the formation of the exterior man. This does not mean that he should entirely abandon the interior life of man. Quite the contrary, for the greatest gifts of the hero are more than prudence, for he must possess a brilliant intellect, an energetic spirit and profound love, self control, perspicacity, and unerring judgment. However, one agrees with Karl Vossler[5] that Gracián places more emphasis on external appearances as a means to reach social and political fame and security than on innate gifts. Thus, *treta* ("stratagem"), image, fabrication, and illusion all come into play in the creation of Gracián's hero, a hero who functions behind the mask of impressiveness and appearances to create the illusion of greatness and power. Primor I advises the candidate from the first that he must be wary, on guard, and self-defensive. He must create the façade of distinction far beyond his true capacity and hide all his strength and true powers so as never to reveal himself completely: familiarity breeds contempt and promotes loss of respect. Gracián's hero, then, is a type of actor—the earth is the stage and the common people are the spectators—who must dazzle, radiate a majestic magnificence, thereby maintaining a super image.

Another avenue to heroism may be found through other exterior methods such as opportunism and mystery, qualities which enhance the hero as a public figure. The hero must be opportunistic in the sense that he should cover up any mistakes, keep good company so as not to blemish his reputation. Another bit of strategy for the calculating hero is to feign some weakness in order to satisfy the envy of his enemies. And the wise hero, above all, will deal opportunistically with Fortune, the mediatrix between the divine and human world. This means that he will be sensitive to her mercurial temperament and will act accordingly, either cautiously or aggressively, depending on her mood. It is most essential, for instance, that the military man be cognizant of his standing with Fortune.[6]

Thus, we find in the portrait of Gracián's hero the highly esteemed merit of *despejo* ("self-confidence"),[7] concomitant with enigma which in itself in Baroque thought constitutes a useful ideal for man. Indeed, the Jesuit's hero is duty bound to project a façade of mystery by constantly mystifying the common folk. A brilliant and astute leader must always dazzle the public not only by fabulous deeds but also by a slow and steady manifestation of his acts and thoughts so as to appear to have inexhaustible powers. And besides being inscrutable, as this ideal man ultimately attempts to dominate the world in the name of God and religion, he must approach life with stoicism. A unique, inaccessible human being, the hero has as his lofty goal to reach the perfection of being the greatest among the great. Stoicism aids him in coping with the frustrations and troubles throughout the course of his endeavors. And a natural companion to stoicism is *simpatía;* that is, the hero-leader must demonstrate a talent plus an unyielding tenacity in influencing and winning over people.

Gracián's keen interest in the development of man's exterior personality of brilliance also concentrates on other angles: *plausibilidad* ("applause") won though the achievement of mighty deeds, both physical and spiritual; a flawless reputation, which can contribute to greater power; a generous and great heart to complement his intellectuality; a fiery and indomitable spirit; the exercise of the Golden Mean as the rule of life. The ideal man is expected to be ambitious, espouse good taste, and, most important, to cultivate novelty and uniqueness as part of his life style. This means that the successful man will break away from prosaic tradition by going beyond the mere imitation of others. He will therefore seek and find fresh alternatives and new interpretations for situations and problems that arise. Finally, the conclusion that the reader will eventually draw from the Jesuit's profile of the ideal man is that the famous Spanish moralist did impose a compendium of rules that were precise, colorful, and often contradictory. It is evident that in this, his first major literary work, Gracián begins to unfold the major ideas that are followed up in his later writings. What Gracián shows us in his first treatise is an affirmation of heroism, based on virtue and pragmatic rules that set forth ideals that perhaps lie far beyond his reach and ours.

II The Politician

As the reader delves into Gracián's second treatise, actually a very brief essay published in 1640 as *El Político, Don Fernando el Católico* (The Politician, Ferdinand the Catholic), he can see how Gracián applies the abstract ideas concerning heroism directly to

Ferdinand, the "happy and universal hero" who is not only the paragon of virtue and heroism in every sense of the word, but also a source of inspiration for contemporary and future leaders in Spain and elsewhere. In this monologue (perhaps it serves as an epilogue to *The Hero*), and with a strong feeling of disenchantment concerning contemporary domestic affairs in Spain, Gracián turns his thoughts toward the grandeur of his country's brilliant past and its superb leader, the King Ferdinand who was frequently cited in *The Hero*. Now in this essay he becomes the protagonist of Gracián's political-historical thoughts. And indeed this monologue represents an outstanding example of imperial eulogy in the Spanish language, an eulogy to the imperial greatness of the famous Spanish king. Following the *topos* of "praise of rulers" and standing witness to the course of national revolts and other national tragedies, Gracián recalls (passionately and perhaps melancholically) the past glories of Spain achieved by Ferdinand of Aragón. Of course, a touch of fervent regionalism on the Jesuit's part is also involved here. Ferdinand is rightly famous for his political prowess and cultural achievements. He united the kingdom, established order, and created a magnificient empire and an era of outstanding institutions and ingenious triumphs.

So it is that Gracián takes it upon himself once again to be a teacher to the world in order to instruct present and future generations. Angel Ferrari has studied *The Politician* within the scheme of an historical, political, and biographical work as in its own way exemplary of the baroque tradition.[8] As a work of historical commentary, Gracián expresses himself from the standpoint of ardent regionalism, praising Aragón as the "mother of heroes." From this regionalistic viewpoint, Gracián moves out toward national and universal concerns. Again his encyclopedic grasp of man and history is impressive.

One may characterize *The Politician* as a long discourse, really a monologue, directed and dedicated to his friend the Duke of Nochera. Gracián even evaluates his own work in *The Master Critic*, citing it as a "precious, small, but unauthorized book" (it was published without the permission of Gracián's superiors). At the beginning and end of the book, in cyclical fashion, the Jesuit is highly conscious of his audience, namely, the duke, whom he addresses directly as he opens and closes the discourse, thereby achieving a classical balance in rhetorical form and style. His knowledge of world history is far-reaching, and he touches on events pertinent to Oriental and Occidental history, including figures from classical antiquity and the Christian world. Much in the style of Pliny and Tacitus, his literary idols, Gracián offers an emotionally charged panegyric to Ferdinand, the perfect man. At the same time, he interweaves domestic and world history, and along with his own political ideals he gives counsel to kings, rulers, and other interested enlightened souls. Thus he effects a fusion of history, biography, and political thought.

What, then, are some of these political ideas? The following are major points in his art of governing:

1. The need of an alliance of crown and throne.

2. Politics should not be confused by *astucia* ("astuteness").

3. The king must possess pragmatic experience as well as a broad education in the Renaissance tradition.

4. The kingdom should not have one center, meaning that there should be no subordination of areas to an all-powerful capital.

5. Divine Providence is the creator of empires.

6. The presence of the king is necessary in the kingdom and in battle as well.

7. It is necessary to elect competent and efficient ministers to help rule: Gracián is a proponent of the delegation of authority.

8. Woman, as wife and mother, plays a significant role in the administration and success of the kingdom. In this work, the Jesuit is uncharacteristically pro-woman and praises Isabella as a unique woman and great leader.

9. The king should make himself indispensable to the kingdom.

10. The king must give commands, not execute them.

11. The height of political greatness lies in *hacer guerra con pólvora sorda* ("to make war with quiet gunpowder," which means to engage in war diplomatically and peacefully).

12. There are no greater enemies than not to have them.

13. A king should never be idle because his actions are always important contributions. His military power rests not only on power but on fame and reputation.

The reader may also read *The Politician* biographically by following the structural lines of the panegyric as observed by Angel Ferrari and Arturo del Hoyo.[9] The work may be divided into five parts: I. The Founding of the Great Spanish Monarchy; II. Designation and Confirmation of Ferdinand as Perfect Founder of the Great Spanish Empire; III. Qualities and Talents of Ferdinand; IV. Cultural and Political Perfections and Contributions of Ferdinand; V. Superior Greatness and Universality of Ferdinand. But most interesting is the fact that this document is an expression of Spanish political theory in the baroque era in which the Jesuit weaves a series of thoughts and rules concerning the *raison d'état*, the modern state and the ruler. The critics Battlori and Peralta[10] view the work as an exemplary example of a baroque work in its fusion of history, political opinion, and biography. Moreover, they see the treatise as an objective correlative of Gracián's literary theory: "*The Politician* is an excellent example of compound, complex, and concealed wit."

III. The Discreet Man

When Gracián published *El discreto* (The Discreet Man) in 1646, he had already published one of his two major works, the first version of *The Mind's Wit*, called *Art of Wit* (1642), and two other works dealing with Renaissance ideal types of figures, *The Hero* (1637) and *The Politician* (1640). Whereas *The Politician* deals with a prototypical figure, Fernando el Católico, both *The Hero* and *The Discreet Man* do not have in mind any specific historical figure; rather, they draw upon numerous individuals, both Spanish and classical, to support the concepts advanced concerning a "perfect" man who would be able to fulfill a higher vision of the human experience. Of course, with the exception of *The Mind's Wit* (and there is unquestionably a relationship between the aesthetic concepts which it advances and a specific moral and ethical vision of mankind), the bulk of Gracián's writings deal with human experience in a pragmatic and almost cynical way. Indeed, Correa Calderón feels, probably correctly, that, whereas the earlier works on Renaissance types are basically optimistic in their approach to human nature, *The Discreet Man*, written at the onset of middle age (Gracián was forty-five when it was published), betrays a far harsher and far more cynical view of mankind.[11] Unquestionably, in both the emphasis on a combination of prescription of pragmatic virtues and denunciation of human failings, *The Discreet Man*, aside from some of the expository correspondences, anticipates the vast panorama of individual and collective humanity developed in the several books of *The Master Critic* beginning in its first part, published in 1651.

While there is little internal evidence to support Correa Calderón's assertion that *The Discreet Man* was written over an extended period of time and that portions of it were presented orally at one or another of the frequent *academias* of the time (forerunners of modern literary salons, *tertulias*, "study clubs"), it is undeniable that the twenty-five *realces* (literally, "highlights"; here, "exemplary chapters") are decidedly miscellaneous in content and in structure.[12] Actually, however, there is a continuity of content, even though it may be difficult to discover an underlying cohesiveness, as we have been able to do in the case of other works which are apparently "structureless," such as *The Mind's Wit*. What continuity or homogeneity that does exist is based, of course, on what already were becoming Gracián's stock moral and ethical pragmatics for societal success and personal fulfillment. On the side of virtues to be subscribed to, we have, for example, an equilibrium between genius and ingenuity (chapter 1: the antithetical pun is more obvious in Spanish: *genio* vs. *ingenio*), mastery or bearing *(señorío)* in one's way of speaking and doing things (chap. 2); patience (chap. 10), the quality of being *en punto*—something combining being "matured to the proper degree" and being the right man at the right time and place (chap. 17). Only one virtue, it would seem, runs somewhat counter to Gracián's emphasis on pragmatic values: in chapter 24 he speaks in defense of an always truthful tongue (what we might now call the Puritan homily about the power of truth and how it will always win out), although one other *realce*, chapter 8, takes up a most interesting defense of ostentation. We note that chapter 8 is the central segment of the work, and it presents a very detailed defense of a quality to be identified with baroque aesthetics as defined and defended by Gracián in *The Mind's Wit;* thus is is a significant segment of *The Discreet Man.*

On the side of denunciations of human weaknesses, we have the admonition not to be uneven (i.e., to be predictable; chap. 6), not to be a buffoon (chap. 9), not to be an opportunist (literally a "joker"—a man, as in cards, who serves whatever cause or purpose is at hand; chap. 11); not to be extravagant in one's behavior (but to see the defense of ostentation; chap. 16). Since these are fairly standard virtues and vices within the content of Gracián's stern portrayal of mankind, there appears to be little need to seek any further underlying coherency for the topics he chooses to discuss in his twenty-five sections. Three passages, however, deserve analysis, since they serve to synthesize strikingly Gracián's thought and to underline the connection between *The Discreet Man*, and his two major works, *The Mind's Wit* and *The Master Critic*. The first passage opens chap. 2, on mastery in speech and actions:

Human nature is such as it was imagined by Hesiodus, Pandora. It was not given wisdom by Palas, nor beauty by Venus; nor did Mercury give it eloquence, and even less Mars valor. But rather art, with careful industry, every day advances it with first this perfection and then with that one. Jupiter did not crown it with that majestic mastery in actions and speech which we admire in some. [Rather], it came from authority attained with accreditation and the control achieved through exercise [i. e., experience]. (p. 81)[13]

What we note first here is the insistence that man is not endowed with virtue by birth (that is, in religious terms, he is not endowed with grace but must earn it through spiritual exercises). Gracián, however, is not interested in religious attainments for man but in how he must, through deliberate, artificial (in the etymological sense of art) application, achieve for himself the image which tradition attributes to the generosity of the gods. It is obvious that the underlying aesthetic of *The Mind's Wit* is reflected here: art is controlled, deliberate artifice rather than inspiration and virtue. One should also note the structure of this passage: this pragmatic, virtually cynical view of human accomplishment is presented in two series of "Not A but B" rhetorical formulas. In each case a vacuous ideal of bounty from on high is rejected in favor of a difficultly won, individually wrought image.

The second passage is from chapter 10, on the "Man of Good Choice":

All human knowledge (if, in the opinion of Socrates, there is anyone who knows anything) is reduced today to making good choices. Little or nothing is invented and in those things that are most important we should be suspicious of any novelty. . . . Hence it is that everyday we see men of subtle ingenuity, of severe judgment, men who are also studious and informed, who, when faced with a choice, become lost. They always choose the worst, letting themselves have what is the worst choice, take pleasure in what is least plausible, to the notice of the wise and the scorn of the rest. Everything turns out unhappily for them and not only do they not win applause, but not even pleasure. They never do anything outstanding and all because they lack the great gift of knowing how to make choices. The fact is that neither study nor ingenuity is enough where choice is lacking. (p. 101)

This is Gracián at his severest. He is not condemning the doltish, mass man, as he so often takes delight in doing, particularly in his allegories, but rather men of otherwise good virtue and intention who waste their chance at excellence, at "discretion," because they lack a pivotal quality. As is the case with so many qualities set up by Gracián for man to follow, choice is not an accidental or fortuitous by-product of the human condition or of other virtues. Rather it is a deliberately won human achievement and jibes well with Gracián's overall belief that the best qualities of man and art are those which are difficult in attainment and comprehension. Note also that this passage, while it lacks the neat rhetorical structure of the first one, begins by rejecting a circumstance in order to affirm that of the virtue involved. Here, what is rejected is the possibility of originality of behavior or human experience—again the illusion of "content" must yield to the necessity for artifice (the ellipses stand for a passage in which Gracián clearly rejects the novel uniqueness of his own age: "We are already at the end of the centuries" [p. 101]).

The third passage is from chapter 19 and concerns good judgment; the Duque de Híjar, don Rodrigo de Silva, is addressing the author:

"Besides being delightful, which is quite the case with this great understanding of objects, and even more so of subjects, of things and of causes, of effects and of emotions, it is also profitable. Its greatest point is in discerning between discreet men and fools, between unique men and common men, toward the choice of intimates. Thus, just as the best thing in cards is knowing when to discard, the greatest rule in living is knowing when to abstract oneself [t. e., rise above a circumstance to contemplate it]." (p. 130)

With this sort of comment we are clearly not dealing with specific vices to be shunned (such as being buffoonish) or virtues to be cultivated (such as knowing when and how to make the right choices) but with synthetic phenomena, the presence of which in a man's character will provide him with personal satisfaction and will set him off both from the masses of common men (the *vulgo*) and from the run-of-the-mill courtier who is lacking so greatly in carefully attained distinction. Gracián reserves for *The Master Critic* his full-scale analysis of mankind and of the society he has created in his image; it is in that vast and panoramic novel that we sense the potential in man for a progressive intensity of "abstraction" and for the achievement of the Island of Immortality, the correlative, in Gracián's fictional universe, of secular intellectual beatification, the inner Empyrean of man's self-realization. But, while *The Discreet Man* in no way approaches either the comprehensiveness or the coherency of *The Master Critic*, the final *realce* is a summary of the sort of life to be led by the self-defined *discreto*. After rejecting various other authoritative life plans, Gracián proposes the following one for analysis:

> But sparing erudite prolixity, the delight was great that was had by that gallant man who divided the comedy [i.e., the Spanish seventeenth-century *comedia*] into three acts and the journey of his life into three seasons. The first season he employed in speaking with the dead [i.e., the books of the ancients], the second, in speaking with the living [i.e., in living life and in storing up experience], and the third, in speaking with himself [i.e., in contemplative retreat]. Let us explain the enigma. (p. 143)

The remaining paragraphs are an exegesis of this enigma or allegorical figure. One notes Gracián's passing insistence, once again, on linking together life (the three seasons) and literature (the three-act comedy and also the role of the authorities in the early formation of man). It is in this final exegesis that Gracián chooses to be pragmatic concerning the overall life of the *discreto;* and, while many of the *realces* anticipate *The Oracle* in title and content, this final segment unquestionably approaches the more creative, "fictitious" structure of *The Master Critic*.

A few more words concerning the *realces*. On the one hand, they are monotonously similar in that each concerns a topic—a vice or a virtue for the would-be *discreto*—which is advanced, analyzed (often with an *exemplum'* where appropriate), and followed by a conclusion, which refers to the deeds and accomplishments of specific contemporary and ancient men. This approach was to be seen in the quote of chapter 19, where what has been an unidentified speaker is identified as the Duque de Híjar and the qualities Gracián has been discussing are attributed to him. Yet, on the other hand, Gracián displays a noteworthy interest in seeking a wide range of formats for the presentation of his twenty-five topics. That is, in the place of the almost unvarying structural format of the *crisis* in *The Master Critic*, here we have straight didactic commentary alternated with personification-allegories, letters by the author to fellow writers, dialogues between the author and other interested parties, so to speak, an attempt at a prose emblem (but without the pictorial component), a fable, apologies, and a panegyric. For example, chapters 1, 2, 4, 5, 10, 12, 15, 24, and 19, which deal with positive values, are called "Eulogy, "Academic Discourse," "Memorandum," "Academic Reasoning," "Encomium," "Apologue," "Problem," "Panegyric," and "Apology." Chapters 3, 6, 9, 11, 20, 14, 16, which are negative in focus, are called "Allegory," "Crisis" (cf. the *crisis*, the chapter divisions of *The Master Critic;* "criticism" or "critical analysis" is to be understood in both cases), "Satire," which is the title of the three chapters 9, 11, 20 (Gracián uses the term in the innocuous sense of "denunciation," without even exaggeration being involved), "Invective," and "Satyricon." It is doubtful whether there is much stylistic variation—e.g., for the purpose of exposition satire is simply the negative counterpart of encomium-apology, and both types of segments are presented in fairly neutral language, with only a sprinkling of the linguistic and intellectual conceits, a dependence upon which would have been made for truer satire, such as that which is found in *The Master Critic*. Nevertheless, the use of an *exemplum* (in chapter 8, for example), the attempt at the more poetic and nondiscursive emblem (chapter 21), and the letters, dialogues, and allegory demonstrate a noteworthy attempt to go beyond the merely essayistic cataloguing of virtues and vices and to move toward the creative representation that forms the structural basis of the later novel.

IV   *El oráculo manual y arte de prudencia*

"Everything is now at its peak, and it is harder than ever to excel.

More is required to make one well-informed today than was needed to make the seven sages of old; and more to deal with one modern man than to treat with a city of people then."[14]

It is with this declaration that Gracián opens his famous *Oracle. A Manual of the Art of Prudence.* This guide for conduct has secured for the Jesuit a prominent place in the tradition of aphoristic literature in the Western world. Since its publication in 1647, the book has had phenomenal success, and perhaps it is easily identified as Gracián's most successful and popular work in terms of its wide international acclaim in its various editions, translations, and studies. The reader can consult, for instance, Correa Calderón's bibliography, which lists a number of translations into French, German, Italian, English, Dutch, Hungarian, Polish, Rumanian, Russian, and Latin.[15] Indeed, the French translation by Amelot de la Houssaye is said to be responsible for Gracián's rise to international fame. It is of interest also to note that Schopenhauer translated the work into German and that the philosopher hailed Gracián as his favorite author. Thus, it is no wonder that the brilliant effort has received so much critical attention. Its three hundred philosophic maxims have influenced not only La Rochefoucauld but La Bruyère and Madame de Sablé[16] as well. Following the general outlines of his former works, Gracián continues to emphasize several of the major themes of his writings: the value of exterior appearances, the power of esteem and influence, the necessity for opportunism, and so on. His bold, analytic mind sets out to teach those special men of life, employing the Horatian ethic of the *utile dulci,* one of the constants in his work. And of course his cynicism and pessimism are all-pervasive in this manual, attitudes of self-defense from which the present-day reader may benefit from some practical advice, based primarily on the key, repetitive words such as caution, suspicion, dissemblance, astuteness, wisdom, deception, and so forth. One word of caution however: Gracián's manual of counsel is not be read as a narrative but rather perused at random as a reference work for profit or pleasure.

As a manifestation of seventeenth-century Spanish humanism, this guide of human conduct recalls other prose works that sought to define the essence of the prince, the courtier, the hero, the politician, and the kind and the wise. It is to be remembered that in seventeenth-century Spain, experiencing an age of definition and redefinition of traditional values, writers like Quevedo and Saavedra Fajardo, to name but two, sought to give insights into the meaning of human existence and the nature of man. And in this epoch of seventeenth-century Europe, an age to be described as the Age of the Maxim, Gracián shared in the quest to deal with the human condition, more specifically, with the condition of the aristocratic and wise man who had to live in a society of seething hostility and who had to struggle to survive and to transcend his fellow man's vulgarity and malice.[17]. As Gracián states his series of moral truths, each followed by a reflective commentary, the reader is once again reminded of the Jesuit's vast erudition and knowledge of classical antiquity and the Christian world—Tacitus, Seneca, Martial, the Bible (e. g., Job 7:1, where life is presented as constant warfare for man).[18]

From a theological point of view, Gracián continues to rely on his formation as a religious and to adhere to Thomistic philosophy. Indeed, like St. Thomas, Gracián maintains that prudence is the highest good for man; it is prudence that is concomitant with wisdom and decisions. Just as St. Thomas thought that prudence was the needed virtue for successful living, so did Gracián adopt the same posture. Arturo del Hoyo,[19] however, finds that Gracián deviated from traditional Thomistic thought in that the *prudencia-solería-experiencia* ("prudence-ingenuity-experience") of St. Thomas becomes for Gracián in *The Oracle prudencia-atención sagaz-desengaño* ("prudence-sagacious attention-disillusionment").

Romera Navarro has dismissed a longtime assumption concerning the manual with his finding that Gracián's friend and patron, Lastanosa, did not compile, edit, and publish *The Oracle*.[20] Rather, Gracián was the sole writer and editor of his own work. But whereas Romera Navarro has only praise for the form and content of the Jesuit's original work, B. B. Ashcom takes grave exception:

Certainly one cannot claim that all of the *Oráculo* is an arid waste. But I cannot feel that Gracián here and elsewhere, measures up to the evaluation that Romera Navarro confers upon him. He lacks the luminous serenity of Montaigne, the tersely humorous candor of Franklin, the lucid, penetrating drive of Bacon, just to mention three of the truly great practitioners of the *arte de prudencia*. Too often his ethic repels, and when we probe his obscure phrase it crumbles into a dusty commonplace.[21]

In the introductory essay to his critical edition of the work, Romera Navarro addresses himself to the point that Gracián's guide of conduct has as its primary goal not to form a man as a paragon of Christian virtue but to form a prudent, wise, and triumphant man in *this* life. Moreover, Romera Navarro stresses the extremely dense prose style of the Jesuit and judges this work to be the most *conceptista* (i. e., using conceits) work in all of Spanish literature. In addition, *The Oracle* is, after all, a truly original work because 228 of the 300 aphorisms expound new ideas, while the remaining seventy-two may be traced back to Gracián's former writings: forty-four maxims from *The Discreet Man;* twenty-three from *The Hero;* two from *The Master Critic;* one from both *The Hero* and *The Discreet Man,* and one that appears in both *The Politician* and *The Discreet Man.*

Other scholarly contributions concerning *The Oracle* include Helmut Hatzfeld's view that the work is both aristocratic and cerebral; this he demonstrates through an analysis of the baroque literary devices such as wordplay, metaphoric expression, concrete versus abstract expression, as well as the use of Spanish proverbs. Hatzfeld also studies other features of the work like allusions and rhymes.[22]. Monroe Hafter finds a new emphasis in *The Oracle,* an emphasis that bespeaks specific stratagems of defense and offense as opposed to the Jesuit's previous proclivities for esoteric generalities. Another refreshing dimension of the book lies in Gracián's counsel on how to adjust to the multitude and *vivir a lo práctico* ("live practically").[23] On the other hand, Olga Prjevalinsky Ferrer discusses the similarities between the Latin Renaissance work by Juan Vives, *Satellitium animi, sine symbole,* and *The Oracle.*[24]

Our own presentation will focus on the structural coherence of Gracián's pragmatic science of wisdom and success. That is to say, when one reads the book he may be overwhelmed by the great body of ideas that are seemingly presented in a chaotic fashion. But indeed, in this rather superficial disorder, there exist underlying general patterns that lend a total cohesiveness to the work. One needs to interpret the systematic ideas of Gracián's aphoristic expressions through the development of the following basic categories of advice: (1) intellectual, (2) social, (3) cultural, (4) practical, (5) moral-ethical-religious, and (6) proverbs.

1. *Intellectual.* Gracián's words of counsel—primarily directed

to leaders of state, rulers, and other worthy gentlemen—are shrewdly welded together with strong notes of pragmatism. Thus, the Jesuit reconciles his own demanding standards with the demands of ordinary life. Nevertheless, in spite of this adherence to practical principles, Gracián does profess an unyielding allegiance to the realm of ideals and the intellect. This means that, in the scale of values, man's intellectuality (genius, inventiveness, and intelligence included) is a means to power, a practical virtue for ordering his life and a precise way to achieve the goal of happiness and success in this life. To sum up his message, the reader need only read the recurring maxims which stress the ideality of man's intellectual powers:

4. Knowledge and courage together make for greatness—the kind of greatness which confers immortality on man.

68. Understanding is a greater gift than memory.

93. A man must be universal. . . . The universal man needs to add to this combination only the culture of good taste and a wide understanding.

100. The valiant man is without illusions: the virtuous is wise; the courtier is philosophical. . . .

247. Give a little more heed to knowing and a little less to doing.

283. To be inventive shows a genius so great as to be touched by madness . . . both genius and judgment—both laudable—are necessary for success.

298. Three things make a prodigy, and they are the greatest gifts that can be given to a man: a fertile mind, a profound judgment and a taste of appreciation of the foibles of life. . . .

2. *Social.* According to Gracián, society is a dismal institution which must be combated defensively; this nonindulgent attitude stands out repeatedly in his writings. His aphorisms concerning society are meant to arm those outstanding men so that they can cope effectively and successfully in their war against their fellowmen. The aphorisms, which subscribe to both positive and negative principles, recommend the cultivation of social graces; the development of an aggressive, extroverted personality; good judgment; and an excellent sense of timing:

11. Cultivate those who can teach you. Let friendly association be a school of knowledge and let conversation teach you culture.

14. Clothe reality with a gracious manner.

20. Keep a clear reputation.

30. Have nothing to do with discredited occupations.
32. Develop a reputation for graciousness.
40. Earn the good will of all.
76. Do not forever be jesting.
77. Know how to adapt yourself to those with whom you deal.
79. Cultivate a jovial character.
86. Avoid becoming an object of gossip.
111. Have friends, for they are second selves.
123. Avoid affectation.
127. Poise should underlie everything.
133. Better mad with all than sane alone, say the politicians. . . . [It] is important to follow the vogue, and it is, sometimes, the greatest wisdom to pretend to folly.
148. Be adept in the art of conversation.
223. Do not be eccentric, either from affectation or through heedlessness.
274. See that you are attractive, for it is the fascination of politic courtesy.

3. *Cultural.* Gracián's demand for culture is the underlying principle of his writings and is most prominent even in this guide for practical living. The need for culture abides eternally in man, and for the Jesuit culture possesses both extrinsic and intrinsic value. It is extrinsic in the sense that man can *use* culture as a means to advance self interests, and it is intrinsic in that culture is a mode of wisdom which leads to truth and greatness:

20. A man must fit the age he lives in.
22. Be supplied with current information.
27. Value intensity more than extensiveness.
28. Be common in nothing, particularly in taste.
65. Elevate your taste . . . [because] cultivated people are known by the refinement of their preferences.
87. See that your knowledge is so well classified that it leads to culture.
203. Know the great men of your century; there are never many.

4. *Practical.* In his code for the aristocrat, Gracián mingles contradictions with a variety of do's and don'ts. His moral code is based essentially on hard-core social realities and therein lies the weaving and interweaving of deviations and paradoxical statements. As one listens to the Jesuit's voice, he becomes conscious that Gracián did firmly believe that principles do have an effect on

human behavior. His brand of social morality is sustained by a utilitarian approach to life as he finds solutions via opportunism, caution, distrust, resourcefulness, all of which are juxtaposed with positive virtues like honesty, diligence, temperance, and good judgment. He allows no room for excesses and, most important, one senses in his writings the conviction that man can be morally successful without necessarily being religious:

5.	Create a feeling of dependence.
7.	Avoid victories over your superior.
31.	Cleave to the fortunate and avoid the unfortunate.
37.	Know how to use sarcasm adroitly.
43.	Think with the few and speak with the many.
67.	Prefer tasks the merit of which can be seen.
107.	Do not be satisfied with yourself.
120.	Live practically.
141.	Do not listen to yourself.
158.	Know how to use your friends.
174.	Do not live in a hurry.

194. Appraise yourself and your affairs conservatively, especially at the start of life.

213.	Learn the art of contradiction. . . .
217.	Do not love or hate forever.
244.	Know how to obligate others.
260.	Do not offer all of yourself to another.
270.	Do not be alone in condemning that which pleases all.

5. *Moral-Ethical-Religious.* An examination of the aphorisms from a moral and ethical point of view mainly reveals that it is through the rational world view, and not the religious, that virtue and success must be sought. However, this secular position does not preclude some religious affirmation, and *The Oracle* does espouse undercurrents of religious sentiment and thought. For example, in aphorism 22 Gracián asserts that "in heaven everything is happiness; in hell everything is sadness." In aphorism 55 he resorts to a Catalonian popular saying in order to define the infinite wisdom and justice of God: "God himself punishes not with a rod but with the fullness of time." In aphorism 3 he pleads for man to "Imitate, then, the Divine way of making people wonder and watch." And in another practical vein in aphorism 296 thoughts and

actions of his hero must be like God in his immensity and infiniteness and "must go clad in transcendent majesty." But it is aphorism 300 that synthesizes, if not the entirety of Gracián's philosophy in *The Oracle*, at least the spirit of his values for a successful way of life:

In a word, be a saint—which is to say everything at once. Virtue is the chain of all perfections, and the center of happiness. It makes a man prudent, alert, sagacious, cautious, wise, valorous, temperate, complete, happy, truthful, and universally heroic. There are three tokens to fortune: health, holiness and wisdom. Virtue is the sun of the world below, and has, for its hemisphere, a good conscience; it is so beautiful that it obtains grace of God and man. . . .

It is significant that the seventeenth-century teachings of Gracián continue to be pertinent to today's world. The virtues stressed are fundamental for all of humanity, virtues that bespeak a basic humanism and rationalism. Success, therefore, encompasses a potpourri of ethics—moral sense, good sense, reason, a reality of self, and so on. What Gracián formulates again and again is that conduct matters more than creed:

8. The man of self-control achieves the greatest height of the soul, for by this self-discipline he avoids common and evanescent impressions.

10. Fortune and Fame: he who suffers from the fickleness of the one may enjoy the permanence of the other.

18. Application and capacity are necessary to the attaining of eminence, and when a man has both, he can accomplish great things.

54. . . . Moral courage is a higher attribute than physical courage.

60. Let your judgments be tolerant.

88. Let all your dealings be upright and noble.

83. Allow yourself some venial weakness, for such a negligence comes to be perhaps the greatest indication of talents.

116. Deal only with honorable folk.

149. Learn to shift blame to others.

181. Do not lie, but do not necessarily tell all the truth.

192. A man of peace is a man of long life.

202. It takes both words and deeds to make the complete man.

280. Be a man of principle.

288. Live for the occasion—the occasion governs everything and will determine all answers.

6. *Proverbs*. This last body of topics indicates that the "popular" does survive to some degree in Gracián thought. Hatzfeld adheres to the idea that Gracián intellectualizes traditional popular sayings.[25] An alternate possibility is that he does not dwell on them in any profound manner and that the proverbs simply form part of Gracián's general cultural background and serve as one more point in support of his statement of the moment. More meaningful, however, is the fact that Gracián's art of living is eloquent evidence that, as the Jesuit reached into the realm of practical human experience, he could not divorce himself from the popular wisdom embodied by the proverbs. His predilection for the proverb recurs in his other works also, thus showing a consciousness of at least some forms of popular culture. Romera Navarro has documented the wide range of proverbs in Gracián's manual,[26] not only from the Spanish tradition but from classical and biblical sources, and these Spanish commonplaces can be found interspersed throughout the work:

16. Science without guidance is doubly madness.

29. Many honor probity but will not themsetves embrace it.

126. You should keep secret your desires, and even more, your defects.

169. Be more careful to avoid a single error than to score a hundred successes.

257. Anyone may be a dangerous antagonist, though few can be worthy friends.

262. The things that are best forgotten are those which are best remembered.

290. Love introduces familiarity and by the road that familiarity comes in, respect goes out!

297. He knows that the walls hear, and that bad acts come back in the end.

V   The Comulgatorio

During the Counter-Reformation Spanish theologians, especially the Jesuits, directed not only the spiritual life of the country but also the intellectual and cultural life. This circumstance was the direct reflection of the strivings by church leaders to reaffirm the strength of traditional Catholicism against the storm of Protestantism that was sweeping northern Europe. Consequently, during Gracián's lifetime in the late Golden Age, religious fanatacism and spiritual intensity reinforced such activities as the Spanish Inquisition, censorship, and the *Index* of prohibited books in Spain. Unquestionably sixteenth- and seventeenth-century Spain produced the richest ascetic and mystic literature in all of Europe. Extraordinary works and authors come to mind: Juan Luis Vives (a friend of Sir Thomas More, Vives spent many years in England; he was basically a nonreligious humanist, although he greatly influenced moralist writers in Spain), Fray Luis de León, Fray Luis de Granada, Pedro Malón de Chaide, St. Ignatius of Loyola, St. Teresa, St. John of the Cross, Quevedo, and many others.

Gracián also shared in these exciting historical moments and religious crosscurrents. Influenced by this milieu and by earlier religious writings like *The Spiritual Exercises* of St. Ignatius, the founder of Gracián's order, and by the very fact of his own commitment to an active religious life, it is no surprise that Gracián's last composition is an important religious work. The *Comulgatorio* (Guide to Pre-Communion Meditation) was published in 1655, three years before his death. As a guidebook to prayer and meditation, the book serves as interesting proof of Gracián's versatility and adds still another dimension to his artistic accomplishments. He dedicates his book to Doña Elvira Ponce de León, Marquesa of Villanueva de Valdueza, and confesses to the reader that this work is his only legitimately published book because it is the only one to have received the proper authorization from his superiors. He also advises the reader that his primary objective is *afecto* ("love") and to it he has subordinated his artful wit (i.e., the aesthetic principles of *The Mind's Wit*). The prologue provides the occasion for other personal commentary on the part of the author: he requests that the user of his guidebook carry it often with him. In addition, he previews its structure: fifty meditations, each following a fixed pattern for the communicant: (1) preparation before Communion, (2) Communion itself, (3) Meditation after Communion, (4) Thanksgiving. But not all of the meditations include four steps and some contain only three steps like Meditations 47, 48, 49, and 50. Nevertheless, it should be noted that the basic situation or role of Gracián is that of the author as preacher. Using a highly emotive style of writing, Gracián articulates his thoughts in order to move the communicant to summits of greatness, but this time in a spiritual rather than in an aesthetic or practical sense.

The complete title of the *Comulgatorio* is *Various Meditations for the Frequent Communicant for the Purpose of Preparation, Reception and Thanksgiving.* Its numerous translations indicate a certain degree of popularity for its religious content at least. Texts appeared in German in 1734, 1738, 1761, and 1847; in Latin, in 1750 and 1753; in Italian in 1675, 1713, 1714, and 1750; and in English in 1875, 1876, and 1900. Romera Navarro is of the opinion that Gracián's fiery and moving language is that of an orator rather than of a writer whose intent is to guide the faithful into the "serenity of silence."[27] But what Gracián does accomplish is to bring biblical experience into a relevant context in the world of the communicant. His purpose derives from an unquestionably ascetic orientation: to help the serious communicant to purify himself for his forthcoming encounter with God in the form of the communion wafer. His posture is to rely on biblical texts for his initial exposition in each meditation. In his prologue he states the obvious fact that he relies on themes from the Old and New Testaments. This broad frame of reference is clear as he alludes to a wide range of biblical figures and events: Christ, Mary, Martha, Mary Magdalen, Joseph, St. Peter, the Apostles, and the doctors of the church. For each meditation, he alternates themes from the Old Testament with those from the New Testament.

It would be of interest to translate various segments from one of the meditations so that the reader can become acquainted with the tone, mood, and style of Gracián's pseudobiblical writing, a writing wrought with emotion and eloquence. His exercises, like those of St. Ignatius of Loyola, follow a pattern: the presentation of the subject and then the meditation so as to bring the powers of mind and soul into an ideal state of being. The final step usually involves a colloquy addressed to the soul or to Christ in a very exclamatory fashion in which a sense of spiritual fullness has been reached with the reception of Christ and a concomitant rejection of sin, all in the spirit of humble thankfulness. Gracián, of course, prescribes daily Holy Communion.

Let us examine Meditation 11, "The Banquet Given by Joseph for His Brothers." *Step One.* After recalling Joseph's situation with his cruel brothers, Gracián proceeds to say:

Soul, who is this true Joseph who was betrayed, abused and mistreated? It is Jesus most loving, kind because he is a brother and venerable because he is the Lord. Who betrayed Him? You, base and ungrateful creature. For how much? For a base reason, a foul pleasure. How? By sinning fearlessly, offending Him so shamelessly. How many times? Every day, every hour and every moment. Be amazed since today you come before His divine presence with greater reason than Joseph's brothers. Here you have not the viceroy of Egypt but the King of Heaven. If the former comes feigning, the Latter comes in hidden ways. If the former gave them wheat, this Lord gives Himself to you in bread. Go before Him recognizing your betrayals before receiving His favors. Ask Him to pardon you before He invites you to partake. Throw yourself at His feet before you sit at His side. Mix your tears with the drink and eat the ash of your penitence with the bread of His gift. (pp. 1034—35)

Step Two. The communicant is asked to dwell on Joseph's great love, which provokes the exclamation:

Oh divine goodness! Oh incomprehensible kindness of Jesus, the -sweetest lamb! The same night that he was vengefully delivered to His enemies, He gives Himself up to His friends in food. He changes bitterness into sweetness and He offers His blood as a toast to those men who contrive to drink of it. And when they grudgingly aspire to take morsels of His, He lovingly gives of Himself in a banquet. With the sweetness of His chalice, he toasts those who prepare gall and vinegar for Him . . . He sweetens with milk and honey those mouths which later will spit in His face. Tell me now, sinner, can any greater ingratitude than yours be imagined, or any greater goodness than that of the Lord? Compare these two extremes and throw yourself at the feet of such a good Brother, admitting your guilt and asking for pardon that cannot be denied you by Him who gives Himself entirely to you in food. (p. 1035)

Step Three. Gracián then refers to Joseph's generosity and to his banquet for his brothers. He continues by saying:

Oh you who sit at the table of the altar . . . take care not to sin again through the commission of new faults. Eat as though you were starving and you will attain the gift, for when the rest perish from hunger, delights will abound for you. Eat with abandon and confidence, for that house and that table being of Jesus, your brother, is yours, who says to you, "I am Jesus whom you betrayed and persecuted. I am not angry but forgiving. Come unto me without fear and place me within you with love." (pp. 1035—36)

Step Four. Recalling the happiness and thanksgiving of Joseph's brothers, Gracián goes on to write:

Soul, you owe more to Him who pardons you. What thanksgiving you should render unto the Lord who so often has pardoned you and seated you at His table! Bear the good news unto the heavenly Father. May the new canticles of your thankfulness reach heaven, repeating again and again your happiness and frequency at the table of the Altar. (p. 1036)

Gracián's doctrine of religious commitment evokes the Platonic trajectory of the four basic stages to reach the ideal. The first is the state of the fall of the soul, with the second being the awareness of the fallen state. The third state brings the longing for redemption, and the final, fourth step consists of achievement—that is, the return of the soul to the ideal from which it has fallen.

Also there is the sense of many of Gracián's themes in his religious treatise. Meditation 9 insists on humility, a topic which he touches upon in *The Master Critic* (X, II); in Meditation, 21 and 36 he decries hypocrisy, another constant in the novel and other works. Meditation 34 is very lyrical as he treats God as the "Celestial Farmer" who sows the divine word in the hearts of men; likewise, Gracián treats the biblical heroines with genuine sensitivity and feeling: the Mother of God in 37, Mary and Martha in Meditation 10, Mary Magdalen in Meditations 21 and 44. At the same time, Meditation 34 is a plea for the cultivation of truth and virtue, a major preoccupation in all of Gracián's writings.

CHAPTER 7

Conclusions

O UR purpose in this book has been to show the content of Gracián's work, a content which indeed reflects baroque anxiety about man's capability to reach perfection and happiness by following Catholic doctrine and, more importantly, by adhering to the nonreligious ethics of Counter-Reformation Spain. Gracián's alternative is for man to be an achiever, to be a person through his own merits and personally achieved perfection. It is unquestionable that the Jesuit demonstrates an aggressive commitment to the human condition and that he was extremely conscious of the time in which he lived. His literary expression, complete with syntatic and linguistic difficulties, can often frustrate the reader in his attempt to grasp the author's meaning. Most of all, the reader will accept the versatility of Gracián, not only in the sense of narrative techniques and imagination but also in his broad frame of reference and in his scholarship and the originality of his thought.

What one finds is that the cardinal dimensions of his literary achievements point to his enormous innovations as a literary theorist, novelist, moralist, and religious writer. As an intellectual he struggled after that which all intellectuals seek—not only a better country, but a better mankind, a better world. Interested in the realities and the issues of the moment conceived within a framework of universal constants, Gracián examined life, its chronic frailties as well as its joys, literature, politics, and, above all, man himself as the chief "actor" of life. We are made aware of a world that is depressing and often absurd, where disorder is more common than normalcy. Nevertheless, the glimpses of hope shine through this pessimistic despair. Man and society can be transformed and redeemed through human efforts and achievements. However, God, the divine, and fate itself play an important and emphatic role in man's shaping of his own life and destiny.

In the case of the works themselves, primarily the structural analysis, it is clear that the *The Mind's Wit* outlines a coherent literary theory which anticipates twentieth-century critical categories for the study of the baroque. And in *The Master Critic*, the reader can witness the mature development of Gracián's philosophy coupled with his artistry as an imaginative writer in this, his only truly fictional work. Again there exists an excellence of structure as found in the underlying motifs of the entire novel and through the patterning of the individual *crisis*.

Finally, it is not surprising that we should find in the essayistic works a unity of concepts in spite of the miscellaneous arrangement of Gracián's ideological principles. In sum, what the modern reader will find in Gracián, aside from the timeless (albeit cynical) wisdom of the ideological treatises, is a writer who demonstrates the creative and intellectual ferment of the baroque, an age which he both described in his allegorical novel and an aesthetics, which he codified and promoted in his critical treatise.

Notes and References

Chapter One

1. More information about the life and times of Gracián can be found in Arturo del Hoyo, *Baltasar Gracián* (Buenos Aires, 1965) and E. Correa Calderón, *Baltasar Gracián su vida y su obra*, 2d. ed. (Madrid, 1970).

2. For the standard works for Golden Age literature see Ludwig Pfandl, *Historia de la literatura nacional española en la Edad de Oro*, trans. J. Rubió Balaguer (Barcelona, 1933), and Ángel Valbuena Prat, *La vida española en la Edad de Oro* (Buenos Aires, 1944).

3. Heinrich Wölfflin, *Renaissance und Barock* (Darmstadt, 1961).

4. See Helmut Hatzfeld, *Estudios sobre el barroco* (Madrid, 1964) and René Wellek, "The Concept of Baroque in Literary Scholarship," in *Concepts of Criticism* (New Haven, 1963), pp. 69—127.

5. See Andrée Collard, *Nueva poesía: conceptismo, culteranismo en la crítica española* (Madrid, 1967). See also Félix Monge, "Culteranismo y conceptismo a la luz de Gracián," in *Homenaje, estudios de filología e historia literaria lusohispanas e iberoamericanas . . .* (La Haya, 1966), pp. 355—81.

6. Cf. the references of note 5.

7. Miguel Batllori in "La vida alternante de Baltasar Gracián en la Compañía de Jesús," *Archivum Historicum Societatis Jesu* 18 (1949), 57, discusses the different humors of Gracián throughout his lifetime. Most predominant is his bilious and choleric temperament.

Chapter Two

1. Leland Chambers' introduction to his translation of Baltasar Gracián, *The Mind's Wit and Art* (Ph.D. dissertation, University of Michigan, 1962), p. 54. All quotations from the *Agudeza* are from

145

Chamber's translation. The second page reference is to the original Spanish text in the *Obras completas*.

2. For example, Luis Carrillo y Sotomayor, in his *Libro de la erudición poética* (Book of Poetic Erudition, 1611), defends *culteranismo;* Francisco Cascales, *Tablas poéticas* (Poetic Tablets, 1617), stresses classical precepts; Juan de Jáuregui, *Discurso poético* (Poetic Discourse, 1623), defends *conceptismo.*

3. Ernst Robert Curtius, *European Literature and the Latin Middle Ages,* trans. Willard R. Trask (New York, 1952), p. 301.

4. Six years before this, in 1642, Gracián published a first edition which appeared under the name of Lorenço Gracián. Its title is different: *Arte de ingenio, tratado de la Agudeza en que se explican todos los modos y diferencias de conceptos* (Art of Ingeniousness, a Treatise on Wit in Which are Explained All Manners and Differences of Conceits). A possible reason for the later change in title is that Gracián wanted to distinguish the second treatise from that of Matteo Pellegrini, *Delle Acutezze* (On Wit, 1639), who accused him of plagiarism. Although our study is not a comparative one, it is worthwhile to observe the essential differences between the two editions which develop the same doctrine of wit. The differences found in the second edition offer a stylistic improvement based on a tighter and more concise sentence structure; architectural rearrangement of the vastly increased number of examples quoted; greater emphasis on writers contemporaneous with Gracián (especially more poets from Aragón); direct reference to the names of sermonizers; Spanish translations of epigrams of Martial by Gracián's friend Manuel de Salinas; the addition of thirteen *discursos;* added judgements on the *culteranista* style, erudition, enigmatic wit, prudent maxims, and wit by means of suspense and surprise; greater emphasis on Gracián's third cause of wit *ejemplar* ("exemplary") through more examples and his enthusiastic comments to the effect that emulation of the ancient masters perfects literary expression; a significant elaboration of poetic truth and imaginative expression by *ingenio.* There is a notable change in the design of the second edition, which is somewhat more logical in its development. Discourse 13, "De la agudeza por desempeño en el hecho" ("On wit by the fulfillment of the fact"), becomes Discourse 45; Discourse 28, "De la agudeza por desempeño en el dicho" ("On wit by the fulfillment of the saying"), becomes 46; and Discourse 30, "De las acciones ingeniosas por invención" ("On ingenious actions by invention"), becomes 47. The order of treatment is further modified as follows:

1642	1648
Wit by difficulty 7	7—8
Similes 8	9—10
Contrasts 14	14—15

Hyperbole 17	19—22
Paradox 18	23—25
Argument 28	26—37
Complex imaginative wit 47	56—57

See Adolphe Coster, "Baltasar Gracián," *Revue Hispanique* 29 (1913), 347—752, especially 621—26; Alberto Navarro Gonzalo, "Las dos redacciones de *La Agudeza*," *Cuadernos de literatura* 4 (1948), 201—14.

5. Marcelino Menéndez y Pelayo, *Historia de las ideas estéticas en España* (Madrid, 1890), II, 356.

6. E. Sarmiento, "Gracián's *Agudeza y arte de ingenio*," *Modern Language Review* 27 (1932), 289—92; 420—29; citation on p. 280.

7. Curtius, p. 298

8. T.E. May, "Gracián's Idea of the *Concepto*," *Hispanic Review* 16 (1950), 15—41; see pp. 16 and 18.

9. S. L. Bethell, "Gracián, Tesauro and the Nature of Metaphysical Wit," *Northern Miscellany of Literary Criticism* 1 (1953), 19—40; quotation from p. 25.

10. F. Maldonado de Guevara, "Del 'Ingenium' de Cervantes al de Gracián," *Anales Cervantinos* 6 (1957), 95—111; quotation from p. 106.

11. Hellmut Jansen, *Die Grundbegriffe des Baltasar Gracián* (Genève, 1958), p. 44.

12. Klaus Heger, *Baltasar Gracián, estilo y doctrina* (Zaragoza, 1960), p. 182.

13. Leland Chambers, p. 2

14. Maldonado de Guevara, p. 101.

15. In *El Discreto* (The Discreet Man, 1646), Gracián distinguishes between *genio* and *ingenio:* "These are the two axes of sagacious brilliance: nature alters them and art enhances them" (p. 78a; our own translation). Arturo del Hoyo clarifies Gracián's position: intellect is the potential in man concerning reason, discretion, and intelligence (*ibid.*, n.1.). Wit is designated as brilliant intelligence and insights which enable one to excel in all the arts and sciences. Gracián says that it belongs to "the sphere of understanding." See Otis H. Green, "El ingenioso hidalgo," *Hispanic Review* 25 (1957), 175—93, and Harold Wienrich, "Das Ingenium Don Quijotes, Ein Beitrag zur literarischen Charakterkunde" (Thesis, University of Münster, 1953).

16. Sarmiento, p. 285.

17. Curtius, pp. 296—97.

18. May, p. 16.

19. Jansen, p. 29 and p. 47.

20. Heger, pp. 182—83.

21. Chambers, p. 82.

22. E. Sarmiento, "On Two Criticisms of Gracián's *Agudeza*," *Hispanic Review* 3 (1935), 23—35; citation from pp. 30—31.

23. May, p. 15.

24. Joseph Mazzeo, "A Seventeenth Century Theory of Metaphysical Poetry," *Romanic Review* 42 (1951), 245—55; quotation from p. 247.

25. Heger, p. 200.

26. E. Correa Calderón, *Baltasar Gracián* (Madrid, 1961), p. 160.

27. Chambers, p. 6.

28. Sarmiento, "Gracián's *Agudeza* . . . ," pp. 287—92; T. E. May, "An Interpretation of Gracián's *Agudeza*," *Hispanic Review* 16 (1948), 291—95; Chambers, pp. 13—21—all briefly study and classify the various types of *agudeza*. Sarmiento in addition gives a general classification of Gracián's ideas in "Clasificación de algunos pasajes capitales para la estética de Baltasar Gracián," *Bulletin Hispanique* 37 (1935), 27—56. One purpose of the present chapter is to organize Gracián's structurally chaotic treatise. Obviously Gracián has followed rhetorical license and a random plan in expressing his ideas. Frequently the terms "agudeza," "ingenio," and "concepto" are interchanged; topics are discussed in an apparently unfixed order. The result is a difficult and complex doctrine with no orderly, obvious pattern.

29. See Anthony Giulian, *Martial and the Epigram in Spain in the XVI and XVII Centuries* (Philadelphia, 1930) and, in particular, "Baltasar Gracián and His Contemporaries," pp. 79—92, in which Giulian discusses Martial's influence upon Gracián, who quotes the Latin epigramist fifty-seven times.

30. Jansen, p. 46, analyzes the term "crisi" as moral and critical censure, using a vituperative, subtle, and prudent wit. He states that it is also used for an ironic or sarcastic observation.

31. Karl Ludwig Selig, in "Gracián and Alciato's *Emblemata*," *Comparative Literature* 8 (1956), 1—11, discusses Gracián's extensive citation of emblems to illustrate types of art. Gracián revered Alciato for the abbreviated style and abstract universal messages in the emblem. Mario Praz, *Studies in Seventeenth Century Imagery* (London, 1939), lists Gracián's *Agudeza* among the emblem books and cites his frequent praise of emblems.

32. See Erasmo Buceta, "La admiración de Gracián por el Infante don Juan Manuel," *Revista de filología española* 11 (1924), 63—66.

33. In many respects, Gracián reveals the influence of the classical rhetorical tradition as it is expressed in the *Rhetorica ad Herennium* (Manual of Rhetoric for Herennius, 1st century, B.C.), the most influential manual of rhetoric in the Western tradition. Curtius also sets Gracián

within the medieval tradition, although recognizing the originality of his approach in his study of agudeza as a discipline for literary creation.

34. For Gracián's strong admiration for individuals and *literati* of Aragón, see J. Mateo and J. Anguiano, "La agudeza y el ingenio aragonés de Gracián," in *Sobre Gracián* (Zaragoza, 1960), pp. 49—57.

35. Edward C. Riley, "Aspectos del concepto de *admiratio* en la teoría literaria del Siglo de Oro," in *Homenaje a Dámaso Alonso* (Madrid, 1963), III, 173—83, includes Gracián as a preceptist who interpreted *admiratio* within the framework of difficult literature by means of mystery and obscurity.

36. See Miguel Batllori, "Gracián y la retórica barroca en España," in *Gracián y el Barroco* (Rome, 1958), pp. 107—14; and Arturo del Hoyo, "Las bases de Gracián," in his edition of Gracián's *Obras completas*, pp. clxiii—clxv, for a discussion of the *Ratio Studiorum* and Gracián's aesthetics.

37. It is interesting to note that Francisco Cascales, in the *Tablas poéticas* (Madrid, 1779), p. 66, treats the subject of *sentencia* in relation to biting wit.

38. Pablo Parada, a Portuguese "general de la artillería" who fought in the siege of Lérida, 1646, and the person to whom Gracián dedicates Part One of *El Criticón*.

39. See Federico Sánchez Escribano, "Gracián ante la comedia española del siglo XVII," *Revista de literatura* 19 (1961), 113—15.

Chapter Three

1. Curtius, *European Literature and the Latin Middle Ages*, p. 296.

2. See Pablo González Casanova, "Verdad y agudeza en Gracián," *Cuadernos americanos*, no. 70 (1953), 143—60.

3. This idea would seem to indicate that Gracián was familiar with Juan Huarte de San Juan's theory on the relationship between the bodily fluids and humors (i.e., temperaments): *Examen de los ingenios para las ciencias* (Madrid, 1575).

4. In the *Oráculo* (The Oracle, 1647), Gracián defends the imagination in the Aristotelian terms of the depiction not only of what was or is but also of what could be.

5. From *El discreto*, in the *Obras completas*, ed. Arturo del Hoyo (Madrid, 1960), p. 101b.

6. Like Aristotle, Gracián sensed that images are the intermediaries between sense and thought, and like St. Augustine, he subordinates imagination to the intellect. Imagination, the most forceful cause of wit, lives in the realm of the emotions and is the neighbor of the passions: "It has its own day and then picks its own occasions, so that it hardly recognizes itself; it becomes transformed with external and even material

impressions; it lives in the confines of the emotion, on the border of the will, and is grudgingly admitted as a neighbor of the passion" *(Agudeza*, p. 512a—b; translation by Leland Chambers, Baltasar Gracián, *Tḥe Mind's Wit and Art* [Ph.D. dissertation, University of Michigan, 1962], p. 896). In all subsequent quotations, the first page reference is to Chambers' translation, while the second is to the *Obras Completas;* see remark on the text of the translation, chapter 2, note 1.

7.   For the concept of imitation in sixteenth-and seventeenth-century Spanish poetry, see Antonio Vilanova Andreu, "Introducción," in *Las fuentes y los temas del Polifemo de Góngora* (Madrid, 1957), pp. 13—43.

8.   Verisimilitude also shares a proximity to truth in the aesthetics of Gracián, especially when it is joined with the art of wit: "Here is the beauty of the art and the boldness of the inventive faculty in finding a means somewhat extravagant, but possible, with which to emerge from the involved labyrinth with delight and profit for whoever reads and whoever hears" *(Agudeza*, pp. 702; 439b).

9.   The *Agudeza* refers to the following *cancioneros* for its quotations from Spanish poetry: *Cancionero de Stuñiga* (15th century), *Cancionero de Hernando del Castillo* (1540, 1557), *Floresta española* (1574), *Flores de poetas ilustres* (1605), *Cancionero de Lastanosa* (1630?), *Las rimas de Lupercio y Bartolomé Argensola* (1632), *Poesías varias de grandes ingenios españoles* (1654), *Romancero general* (1600, 1604, 1605), and *Cancionero de 1628.* José Blecua has edited the *Poesías varias de grandes ingenios españoles* (Zaragoza, 1946). Like Miguel Romera Navarro, he affirms in "Dos aprobaciones de Gracián" *(Hispanic Review*, vol. 8 [1940]), that Gracián was the collector of this anthology, known also as the *Cancionero de Alfay* (Songbook of Alfay).

10.   *Oráculo*, ed. cit., p. 179b, "105. *No cansar*" ("Do not tire").

11.   See Dámaso Alonso, *Góngora y el Polifemo* (Madrid, 1961), I, 11—257; and Susan Kirk, "Relaciones entre la poesía de Sor Juana Inés de la Cruz y la de los poetas del Renacimiento y Barroco en España" (Ph.D. dissertation, University of Missouri, 1964), pp. 1—11.

12.   In *The Master Critic* there are several references to the need for erudition in man's life: "Di en leer, comencé a saber y a ser persona . . . " ("I began to read, I began to know and to be a person"), quoted from the edition of Miguel Romera Navarro [Philadelphia, 1938], I, 46). In *The Oracle*, Gracián observes: "Hombre sin noticias, mundo a oscuras" ("A man without news, a world in darkness") *(ed. cit.*, p. 152a). In *The Discreet Man*, we read: "La noticiosa erudición es un delicioso banquete de los entendidos" ("Informed erudition is a delicious banquet for those in the know") *(ed. cit.*, p. 92b).

13.   With regard to erudition, it is necessary to mention one extraliterary

factor: Gracián's close association with his patron Don Vicencio Juan de Lastanosa and the literary circle in Huesca, Aragón, a center of learning. Gracián had access to Lastanosa's library, which was one of the richest in seventeenth-century Spain. In *The Master Critic*, Part Two, Crisi II, Gracián describes the magnificent library of his patron, who was a great antiquarian and humanist. See Ricardo del Arco Garay, *La erudición aragonesa en el siglo XVII en torno a Lastanosa* (Madrid, 1934); and E. Correa Calderón, "Lastanosa y Gracián," in *Homenaje a Gracián* (Zaragoza, 1958), pp. 65—76.

14.   As Curtius points out, "Gracián's historical and esthetic position in respect to the ancients and moderns bears no relation to the French *Querelle des Anciens et des Modernes*" (p. 298). Emilio Carilla presents an opposing view. In his article, "Antiguos y modernos en la literatura española," *Anuario de filología* 4 (1965), 195—216, he affirms that such a battle did exist in seventeenth-century Spain. For mention of Gracián, see pp. 211—16.

15.   Examples are numerous. For instance, "There is a culture of taste, as well as of art. Both together are brothers of the same womb, sons of ability, heirs equally to excellence" *(El héroe,* in *Obras completas* p. 13a); "There is no perfection without choice. Two advantages obtain: the ability to choose and to choose well" *(El discreto,* in *Obras completas,* p. 228a); "Concerning taste I have heard it said always that there can be no argument . . . ; everyone has his own taste and every taste has someone" *(Criticón,* in *ed. cit.,* I, 285). All translations are our own.

16.   Karl Borinski, *Gracián und die Hofliteratur in Deutschland* (Halle, 1894).

17.   Maldonado de Guevara, "Del 'Ingenium' de Cervantes al de Gracián," *Anales Cervantinos* 6 (1957), 97—111; see p. 111 in particular.

18.   Coster sees Gracián's influence on the French Jesuit Dominique Bouhours in the formation of the *je ne sais quoi* in the latter's *Les Entretiens d'Artiste et d'Eugène* (The Conversations of the Artist and Eugène). See Adolphe Coster, "Baltasar Gracián," *Revue hispanique,* 19 (1913), 347—752; see in particular "Gracián hors d'Espagne. En France," pp. 666—85.

19.   Alberto Porqueras-Mayo, "Función de la fórmula 'no sé qué' en textos literarios españoles (siglos XVIII—XX)," *Bulletin hispanique,* 67 (1965), 253—73.

20.   Numerous critics have noted the many literary preferences of Gracián. The following have been helpful in the present examination: Coster, pp. 637—49; José María Cossío, "Gracián, crítico literario," *Boletín de la Biblioteca Menéndez Pelayo* 5 (1923), 69—74; E. Correa Calderón, *Baltasar Gracián* (Madrid, 1961): "Teoría y estética de la *Agudeza,*" pp.

154—68; I. Mateo and J. Anguiano, "La agudeza y el ingenio aragonés de Gracián," in *Sobre Gracián* (Zaragoza, 1960), pp. 49—57; and Chambers, pp. 21—29.

21. Cossío, p. 74.

22. Curtius, pp. 298—301.

23. Chambers, p. 21.

24. Chambers, p. 24.

25. See Karl Ludwig Selig, "Gracián and Alciato's *Emblemata*," *Comparative Literature* 8 (1956), 1—11.

26. For the importance of the sermon in sixteenth-and seventeenth-century Spain see Miguel Herrero García, *Sermonario clásico* (Madrid-Buenos Aires, 1942).

27. Federico Sánchez Escribano, "Gracián ante la comedia española del siglo XVII," *Revista de literatura* 19 (1961), pp. 113—15; p. 113 in particular.

28. Cossío, p. 73.

29. Correa Calderón, *Baltasar Gracián* . . . , p. 265.

30. Adolphe Coster, "Baltasar Gracián," *Revue Hispanique* 29 (1913), 347—752; p. 638 in particular.

31. For critical interpretations of the Spanish baroque, see Helmut Hatzfeld, *Estudios sobre el barroco* (Madrid, 1964), and Dámaso Alonso, I, 11—257.

32. See Alberto Porqueras-Mayo, *El prólogo como género literario* (Madrid, 1957), p. 111. Likewise Porqueras-Mayo notes that intimate contact is established in the prologue of *El héroe* when Gracián addresses the cultured reader, "How especially do I want you!" (p. 159; our own translation).

33. The reader is addressed also on pp. 296a, 296b, 356b, 368b, 373a, among others.

34. Wylie Sypher, *Four Stages of Renaissance Style* (New York, 1955), pp. 201—19.

35. See Carl J. Friedrich, *Age of the Baroque, 1610—1660* (New York, 1952), chapter 2, "Baroque in Life and Letters."

36. See Curtius, pp. 293—301.

37. For an extensive study of the "a lo divino" tradition, see Bruce W. Wardropper, *Historia de la poesía lírica a lo divino en la cristiandad occidental* (Madrid, 1958).

38. Heinrich Wölfflin, *Principles of Art History*, trans. M. D. Hottinger (New York, 1949).

39. A religious interpretation of the baroque is given by Stephen Gilman, "An Introduction to the Ideology of the Baroque in Spain," *Symposium*, 1 (1946), 82—107.

Chapter Four

1. Baltasar Gracián, *El Criticón* in his *Obras completas*, edited by Arturo del Hoyo (Madrid, 1960). All quotations in this and the next chapter will be from this edition and are followed by part and page references. All translations are our own.

2. In Jorge Luis Borges, *A Personal Anthology* (New York: Grove Press, 1967), pp. 84—85.

3. Marcelino Menéndez y Pelayo, *Orígenes de la novela* (Madrid, 1962), I, 81—84.

4. José Montesinos, "Gracián o la picaresca pura," *Cruz y raya* 4 (1933), 37—40.

5. Miguel Romera Navarro, "En torno a la obra maestra," in *Estudios sobre Gracián* (Austin, Texas, 1950), pp. 27—44. See also Joseph R. Jones, "From Abraham to Andrenio: Observations on the Evolution of the Abraham Legend, Its Diffusion in Spain and Its Relation to the Theme of the Self-Taught Philosopher," *Comparative Literature Studies* 6 (1969), 69—101.

6. Miguel Romera Navarro, "Autores latinos en *El Criticón*," *Hispanic Review* 2 (1934), 103—33.

7. Antonio Prieto, "El sujeto narrativo en *El Criticón*," in his *Ensayo semiológico de sistemas literarios* (Barcelona, 1972), pp. 189—253.

8. See Del Hoyo, "Estudio preliminar," in *B. Gracián*, pp. CCVII—CCXXXV.

9. See Robert D. F. Pring-Mill, "Some Techniques of Representation in the *Sueños* and the *Criticón*," *Bulletin of Hispanic Studies* 45 (1968), 270—84.

10. Klaus Heger, *Baltasar Gracián, estilo y doctrina* (Zaragoza, 1960), pp. 107—114; summarizes different critical opinions of Gracián's Christianity.

11. See Edward Sarmiento, "A Preliminary Survey of Gracián's *Criticón*," *Philological Quarterly* 18 (1933), 235—54.

12. Translation taken from Otis Green, *Spain and the Western Tradition* (Madison: University of Wisconsin Press, 1966), II, 16—17.

13. See Monroe Z. Hafter, *Gracián and Perfection* (Cambridge: Harvard University Press, 1966), pp. 156—59.

Chapter Five

1. Miguel Romera Navarro, "Las alegorías del *Criticón*," in his *Estudios sobre Gracián* (Austin, Texas, 1950), pp. 71—102.

2. For the meaning of the word *crisi* see Otis H. Green, "On the Meaning of *Crisi* before *El Criticón*," *Hispanic Review* 21 (1952), 218—20.

3. See Paul Ilie, "Gracián and the Moral Grotesque," *Hispanic Review* 39 (1971), 30—48, as well as José Camón Aznar, "El monstruo en Gracián y en Goya," in *Homenaje a Gracián* ed. Charles V. Aubrun (Zaragoza, 1958), pp. 57—63. Gerhardt Schröder also studies the monstrous in *Graciáns "Criticón"* (Munich, 1966), pp. 172—87.

4. All quotations in the following pages are taken from the translation by Leland C. Chambers, "Baltasar Gracián's *The Mind's Wit and Art*" (Ph.D. dissertation, University of Michigan, 1962).

5. See note 1.

6. See Karl Ludwig Selig, "Gracián and Alciato's *Emblemata*," *Comparative Literature* 8 (1956), 1—11. Gerhardt Schröder also relates emblems and the ideas of Alciato and Bosch to Gracián.

7. See Benito Sánchez Alonso, "Sobre Baltasar Gracián (notas linguoestilísticas)," *Revista de filología española* 45 (1962), 161—225. Other valuable studies on style include Francisco Ynduráin, "Gracián, un estilo," in *Homenaje . . .*, ed. Charles V. Aubrun, pp. 163—88; and José Manuel Blecua, "El estilo de Gracián en *El Criticón*," *Archivo de filología aragonesa* 1 (1945), 7—32.

8. The importance of Lastanosa has been studied by E. Correa Calderón, "Lastanosa y Gracián," in ed. *Homenaje . . .*, Charles V. Aubrun, pp. 65—76, and by Karl Ludwig Selig, *The Library of Vicencio Juan de Lastanosa* (Genève, 1960).

9. See Robert Pring-Mill, "Some Techniques of Representation in the *Sueños* and the *Criticón*," *Bulletin of Hispanic Studies* 45 (1968), 270—484.

10. Gracián's shift from "imitation" to "creation" is discussed by Miguel Batllori, "Gracián y la retórica barroca en España," in *Gracián y el barroco* (Roma, 1958), pp. 107—14.

Chapter Six

1. Machiavelli's influence on Gracián has been a controversial subject among critics. For instance, Werner Krauss says that Gracián is pro-Machiavelli in *La doctrina de la vida según Baltasar Gracián* (Madrid, 1963), pp. 70—73 and 118—20. Other critics like E. Correa Calderón are of the opinion that Gracián is unquestionably anti-Machiavelli: *Baltasar Gracián, su vida y su obra* (Madrid, 1970), pp. 129, 148, and 269.

2. Consult Alberto Porqueras-Mayo, *El prólogo como género literario* (Madrid, 1957), p. 133.

3. Monroe Z. Hafter, *Gracián and Perfection, Spanish Moralists of the Seventeenth Century* (Cambridge, Mass., 1966), pp. 110—11.

4. See Otis Green, "On the Attitude Toward the *vulgo* in the Spanish Siglo de Oro," *Studies in the Renaissance* 4 (1957), 190—200.

5. Karl Vossler, *Literatura española. Siglo de oro* (México, 1941), pp. 100—101.

6. See Otis Green, *Spain and the Western Tradition* (Madison, Wisc., 1966), II, 290, as well as Klaus Heger, *Baltasar Gracián: estilo y doctrina* (Zaragoza, 1960), pp. 83—102.

7. For this and other key concepts see chapter 8 of Werner Krauss, pp. 256—286.

8. Angel Ferrari, *Fernando el Católico en Baltasar Gracián* (Madrid, 1945).

9. Arturo del Hoyo, in *Baltasar Gracián, "Obras completas"* (Madrid, 1960), pp. CXXXIX—CXL.

10. Miguel Battlori and Ceferino Peralta, *Baltasar Gracián en su vida y en sus obras* (Zaragoza, 1969), pp. 65—75.

11. Correa Calderón, pp. 168—71.

12. The only separate study on the *Discreto* concerns the prologue, which ties the twenty-five miscellaneous segments together: See Joseph R. Jones, "Topoi of Dedication in the Prologues of Gracián's *Discreto* and Guevara's *Década*," *Romance Notes* 7 (1965), 54—57.

13. Page references are to the Spanish text in the *Obras completas*. All translations are our own. Although an English translation exists, with several eighteenth-century printings (see Bibliography), the looseness of its rendition of the original Spanish indicated the advisability of fresh translations.

14. All quotations are taken from the translation of the *Oráculo, The Science of Success and The Art of Prudence*, trans. Lawrence C. Lockley (San Jose, Cal., 1967).

15. Correa Calderón, pp. 326—408.

16. See Graydon Hough, "Gracián's *Oráculo Manual* and the *Maximes* of Mme. de Sablé," *Hispanic Review* 4 (1936), 68—72.

17. See Krauss, pp. 159—74.

18. Hafter, p. 150.

19. Arturo del Hoyo, p. CLVII.

20. Miguel Romera Navarro, in Baltasar Gracián, *Oráculo manual y arte de prudencia* (Madrid, 1954), pp. VIII—XXXVII.

21. B. B. Ashcom, review of the volume in note 20, *Hispanic Review* 25 (1956), 164.

22. Helmut Hatzfeld, "El barroquismo del *Oráculo manual* de Gracián," in his *Estudios sobre el barroco* (Madrid, 1964), pp. 345—62.

23. Hafter, p. 151.

24. Olga Prjevalinsky Ferrer, "De lo renacentista y de lo barroco en las máximas morales de Vives y de Gracián," *Hispanófila* 7 (1959), 19—28.

25. Hatzfeld, pp. 352–54.
26. These appear throughout Romera's edition of the *Oráculo*.
27. As quoted by Correa Calderón, p. 198.

Selected Bibliography

PRIMARY SOURCES

1. Complete works (in chronological order; there are many more imprints than these listed; they have been chosen to suggest the geographical diffusion of the works).

Obras de Lorenzo Gracián. . . . Madrid: En la Imprenta Real, 1663. Also issued in 1674.

Obras de Lorenzo Gracián. . . . Madrid: Pablo de Val, 1664.

Obras (Barcelona: J. Suriá y Antonio Lacavalleria, 1667. Also issued in 1669, 1683).

Obras de Lorenzo Gracián. Amberes: Geronymo y Juan Bautista Verdussen 1669. Also issued in 1700, 1725.

Obras de Lorenzo Gracián. . . . Amberes: Henrico y Cornelio Verdussen, 1702.

Obras de Lorenzo Gracián. . . . Madrid: Antonio de Reyes, 1720.

Obras de Lorenzo Gracián. Madrid: Pedro Marín, 1773.

Obras completas. Introducción, recopilación y notas de E. Correa Calderón. Madrid: Aguilar, 1944.

Obras completas. Estudio preliminar, edición, bibliografía y notas de Arturo del Hoyo. Madrid: Aguilar, 1960. This is called the "2. ed.," and there is a "3. ed." dated 1967.

Obras completas. Edición y estudio preliminar de Miguel Batllori y Ceferino Paralta. Madrid: Atlas, 1969–. Biblioteca de Autores Españoles, nos. 229–.

2. Separate Works

    a. *Agudeza y arte de ingenio* (in chronological order)

    Agudeza y arte de ingenio, en que se explican todos los modos, y diferencias de concetos. . . . Huesca: Juan Hogues, 1648. Enlarged edition published with same imprint, 1649.

    Agudeza y arte de ingenio. Prólogo de Eduardo Ovejero y Maury. Madrid: Biblioteca de Filósofos Españoles, 1929.

Agudeza y arte de ingenio. Buenos Aires: Espasa-Calpe, 1942. Reprinted, 1944, 1945, 1957.

Agudeza y arte de ingenio. Nota preliminar de F.S.R. Revisión y notas de E. Correa Calderón. Madrid: Aguilar, 1944.

Agudeza y arte de ingenio. Edición, introducción y notas de Evaristo Correa Calderón. Madrid: Castalia, 1969.

b. *Arte de ingenio* (first version of preceding title; in chronological order)

Arte de ingenio, tratado de la agudeza. Madrid: Juan Sánchez, 1642.

Arte de ingenio, tratado de la agudeza. Lisbon: Na Officina Craesbeeckiana, 1659.

Arte de ingenio, tratado de la agudeza. Amberes: Jerónimo y Juan Bautista Verdussen, 1669.

c. *El comulgatorio* (in chronological order)

El comulgatorio. Contiene varias meditaciones para que los que frequentan la Sagrada Comunión, puedan prepararse, comulgar y dar gracias. Zaragoza: Juan de Ybar, 1655.

Meditaciones . . . para y después de la Sagrada Comunion. Valencia: Joseph García, 1739.

Meditaciones para antes y despúes de la Sagrada Comunion. Madrid: Andrés de Sotos, 1787.

Manual eucarístico o meditaciones varias para antes y después de la Sagrada Comunión. Madrid: Apostolado de la Prensa, 1928.

El comulgatorio. Madrid: Aguilar, 1958.

d. *El criticón* (in chronological order)

El criticón. Zaragoza: Juan Nogues, 1651—1653. Parts One and Two respectively; latter issued in Huesca.

El criticón. Lisbon: En la oficina de Henrique Valente de Oliveira, 1656; 1657; 1661. Issued in three separate parts.

El criticón. Madrid: Pablo de Val, 1658—1657 [sic]. Parts One and Three, respectively.

El criticón. Barcelona: Antonio Lacavelleria, 1664. Parts Two and Three. Also issued in 1682.

Tres partes de El criticón. Barcelona: Antonio Lacavelleria, 1664. Also issued in 1682.

El criticón. Edición transcrita y revisada por Julio Cejador, con prólogo (Madrid: Renacimiento, 1913—14).

El criticón. Edición crítica, comentada por M. Romera-Navarro. London: Oxford University Press, 1938—40.

El criticón. Selección, estudio y notas por José Manuel Blecua. Zaragoza: Ebro, 1950. 2. ed., 1956.

El criticón. Estudio, notas y comentario de textos de Antonio Prieto. Madrid: Ediciones Iter, 1970.

El criticón. Edición, introducción y notas de Evaristo Correa Calderón. Madrid: Espasa-Calpe, 1971.

e. *El discreto* (in chronological order)

El discreto. Huesca: Juan Nogues, 1646. Reprinted in 1647.

El discreto. Barcelona: Pedro Juan Dexen, 1647.

El discreto. Coimbra: Na Officina de Thomé de Carvalho, 1656.

El discreto. Amsterdam: En Casa de Pedro Le Grand, 1665.

El discreto. Madrid: Hernando, 1911. Several reprintings.

El discreto. Texto crítico por Miguel Romera Navarro y Jorge M. Furt. Buenos Aires: Academia Argentina de Letras, 1960.

El discreto. Edición, prólogo y notas de Arturo del Hoyo. Madrid: Aguilar, 1963.

f. *El héroe* (in chronological order)

El héroe. Madrid: Diego Díaz, 1639.

El héroe. Lisbon: Manuel de Sylva, 1646.

El héroe. Amsterdam: En Casa de Juan Blaeu, 1659.

El héroe. Coimbra: Thomé de Carvalho, 1660.

El héroe. Reimpresión de la edición de 1639, publicada con las variantes del códice inédito de Madrid . . . por Adolphe Coster. Chartres: Librairie Lester, 1911.

g. *Oráculo* (in chronological order)

Oráculo manual y arte de prudencia. Madrid: María de Quiñones, 1653.

Oráculo manual y arte de prudencia. Lisbon: Henrique Valente de Oliveira, 1657.

Oráculo manual y arte de prudencia. Amsterdam: En Casa de Juan Blaeu, 1659.

Oráculo manual y arte de prudencia. Edición de Gabriel Juliá. Heidelberg: C. Winter, 1946.

Oráculo manual y arte de prudencia. Edición, estudio preliminar y notas de Arturo del Hoyo. Madrid: Castilla, 1948.

Oráculo manual y arte de prudencia. Edición crítica y comentada por Miguel Romera Navarro. Madrid: Consejo Superior de Investigaciones Científicas, 1954.

Oráculo manual y arte de prudencia. Edición facsímil por Jorge Furt. Buenos Aires: Coni, 1959.

Oráculo manual y arte de prudencia. Edición, introducción y notas de E. Correa Calderón. Salamanca: Anaya, 1968.

h. *Poesías varias de grandes ingenios españoles* [attributed to Gracián] (in chronological order)

Poesias varias de grandes ingenios españoles. Recogidas por Joseph
   Alfay i dedicadas a Don Francisco de la Torre. . . . Zaragoza:
   Juan de Ibar, 1654.

Poesias varias de grandes ingenios españoles. . . . Edición y notas de
   [José Manuel Blecua]. Zaragoza: Consejo Superior de
   Investigaciones Científicas, 1946.

i. *El político* (in chronological order)

El político D. Fernando el Catolico. Zaragoza: Diego Dormer, 1640.

El político D. Fernando el Catholico. Huesca: Juan Nogués, 1646.

El político D. Fernando el Catholico. Amsterdam: En Casa de Juan
   Blaeu, 1659.

El político don Fernando el Católico. Edición facsímil. Zaragoza:
   Consejo Superior de Investigaciones Científicas, Institución Fernando el Católico, 1953.

El político. Introducción de E. Tierno Galván; edición y notas de E.
   Correa Calderón. Salamanca: Anaya, 1961.

3. Selected Works (in chronological order)

Páginas escogidas. Selección y notas de Luis Santamarina. Barcelona: Luis
   Miracle, 1932.

Baltasar Gracián. Estudio preliminar y selección de textos [por] J. García
   López. Barcelona: Labor, 1947.

Pensamientos de Baltasar Gracián. Selección y notas de Antonio G. Gavaldá
   Barcelona: Sintes, 1957.

4. Translations into English of the *Agudeza*

Baltasar Gracián's *The Mind's Wit and Art.* Translated by Leland Hugh
   Chambers. Ph.D. dissertation, University of Michigan, 1962.

5. Translations into English of *El criticón*

The Critick. Written originally in Spanish by Lorenzo Gracian one of the
   best wits of Spain and translated into English by sir Paul Rycaut. Esq.
   London: Printed by T. N. for Henry Brome at the Gun in St. Paul's
   Churchyard, 1681.

6. Translations into English of *El discreto*

*The complet gentleman, or a description of the several qualifications, both
   natural and acquired, that are necessary to form a great man.* Written
   originally in Spanish and now translated into English [by T. Saldkeld].
   London: Printed for W. Whitestone?, 1730. Reprinted, Dublin:
   Printed for W. Whitestone?, 1760. Also issued in 1776.

7. Translations into English of *El héroe* (in chronological order)

The Heroe. Translated by Sir John Skeffington London: Printed for John
   Martin and James Allestrye . . . , 1652.

The Hero. With remarks . . . of . . . J. Courbeville. Translated by a

Gentleman of Oxford. Dublin: Risk, 1726. Also issued with imprint of London: Printed by R. Cox, 1726.

8. Translations into English of the *Oráculo* (in chronological order)

The Courtiers Manual Oracle or The Art of Prudence. Now done into English [based on the French translation by Amelot]. London: Swalle, 1694. Also published as

The Art of Prudence; or a Companion for a Man of Sense. Made English and Illustrated with the Sieur Amelot de la Houssaie's Notes, by Mr. Savage. London: J. Bowyer, 1702. Reprinted in 1705 and 1714.

The Art of Worldly Wisdom by Baltasar Gracián. Translated from the Spanish by Joseph Jacobs. London-New York: Macmillan, 1892. Reprinted in 1904, 1913, 1920, 1943, 1944, 1945, 1946, and 1950.

A Truthtelling Manual and the Art of Worldly Wisdom, Being a Collection of the Aphorisms which Appear in the Works of Baltasar Gracián. Translated by M. Fischer. Springfield, Ill.: C. Thomas, 1934. Reprinted in 1942, 1945, and 1957.

The Art of Worldly Wisdom. Translated by Otto Eisenschmil. New York: Essential Books, 1947.

The Oracle. A Manual of the Art of Discretion. Oráculo manual y arte de prudencia. The Spanish Text and a New English Translation, with Critical Introduction and Notes by L. B. Walton. London: J. M. Dent and Sons, 1953. Reprinted in 1962.

The Art of Worldly Wisdom. Translated from the Spanish by Joseph Jacobs. New York: F. Ungar, 1960.

The Science of Success and the Art of Prudence. Translated by Lawrence C. Lockley. San José, Calif.: University of Santa Clara Press, 1967.

9. Translations in English of Selections

The Best of Gracián. A New Translation by Thomas C. Corvan. New York: Philosophical Library, 1964.

See also items three and four of preceding section.

SECONDARY SOURCES

ARCO GARAY, RICARDO DEL. "Baltasar Gracián y los escritores conceptistas." In *Historia general de las literaturas hispánicas*, edited by Guillermo Díaz Plaja. Barcelona: Barna, 1949—58, III, 629—724. Studies Gracián, his writing and literary theory from a regionalistic point of view.

BATLLORI, MIGUEL. *Gracián y el barroco* Roma: Edizioni di Storia e Letteratura, 1958. A general study of Gracián, the man and the writer, using his own life and the baroque as the principal points of reference.

BELL, AUBREY. *Baltasar Gracián.* Oxford: Oxford University Press, 1921.

Biographical-historical study with some observations on Gracián's artistic ideas.

BETHELL, S. L. "Gracián, Tesauro and the Nature of Metaphysical Wit." *Northern Miscellany of Literary Criticism* 1 (1953), 19—40. Sees Gracián as a practical critic of wit and studies his theory of conceits.

BLECUA, JOSÉ MANUEL. "El estilo de Gracián en *El Criticón.*" *Archivo de filología aragonesa* 1 (1945), 7—32. A discussion of the allegorical and baroque style of the novel.

CASSOU, JEAN. "Baltasar Gracián" *Mercure de France* 172 (1924), 521—28. Finds that Gracián's *conceptista* theory shows a similarity to, and an influence on, Baudelaire's theory of correspondences.

CHAMBERS, LELAND H. "Baltasar Gracián's *The Mind's Wit and Art*". Ph.D. Dissertation, University of Michigan, 1962. An excellent translation of the *Agudeza*, with a valuable introduction that defines the work as baroque in both structure and organizational form.

————. "Theory and Practice in the *Agudeza y arte de ingenio.*" In *Litterae hispanae et lusitanae*, edited by Hans Flasche. München: Max Hueber, 1968, pp. 109—17. In the *Agudeza*, Gracián put into practice some of his dicta regarding the nature of beauty, variety, erudition, and difficulty.

CORREA CALDERÓN, EVARISTO. *Baltasar Gracián, su vida y su obra;* 2 ed. aum. Madrid: Gredos, 1970, orig. 1961. Biographical details of Gracián's life and some analyses of his works.

COSTER, ADOLPHE. "Baltasar Gracián." *Revue hispanique* 29 (1913), 347—752. Also published as *Baltasar Gracián.* Zaragoza: Institución Fernando el Católico, 1947. An analytical study that treats Gracián as a paradoxical critic inconsistent in his use of the terms "agudeza" and "concepto."

CROCE, BENEDETTO. *I trattisti italiani del concettismo e Baltasar Gracián.* Napoli: Regia Università, 1899. Considers that Gracián's concept of *gusto* represents a modern intuitive value judgment for literature and finds that his literary criticism reflects seventeenth-century preciosity rather than literary theory.

FABILLI, JOSEPHINE C. "A Study of Baltasar Gracián's *El Criticón:* Sources and Selected Themes." *Dissertation Abstracts* 31 (1970), 354A—55A (USC). "After a discussion of Gracián's life, writings and influence, two subjects receive emphasis. . . .[The] first subject [concerns] a possible Arabic source of the novel. . . . The second matter treated . . . is Gracián's view of women in his philosophical novel [*El Criticón*]" (from the abstract).

FOSTER, VIRGINIA RAMOS. "Baltasar Gracián y los conceptos de la poesía antes de la *Agudeza y arte de ingenio.*" *Hispanófila*, no. 35

(1969), 33—43. A descriptive study of the major literary theoreticians and their concepts of poetry before the *Agudeza*.

————. *Literary Ideas of Baltasar Gracián*. Ph.D. Dissertation, University of Missouri, 1966. A comprehensive profile of Gracián's aesthetics as found in the *Agudeza* and *El Criticón*.

————. "Nota sobre la *Agudeza y arte de ingenio* y la estética barroca." *Revista de ideas estéticas* 26 (1968), 167—71. Also as "A Note on Gracián's *Agudeza y arte de ingenio* and Baroque Esthetics." *Romance Notes* 11, no. 3 (1969), 611—16. Stresses how the major concepts in contemporary discussions on the baroque are to be found in the *Agudeza*.

————. "The Status of Gracián Criticism: a Bibliographic Essay," *Romanistisches Jahrbuch* 18 (1967), 296—307. A survey of the major issues in Gracián scholarship.

GARIANO, M. C. "Simbolismo y alegoría en *El Criticón* de Gracián." *Asomante*, 22, no. 2 (1966), 39—50. The *Criticón* is classified as an allegorical novel by virtue of its extensive use of allegory, its moral-satirical intent, and its concern for the historical and theological destiny of man.

GONZÁLEZ CASANOVA, PABLO. "Verdad y agudeza de Gracián." *Cuadernos americanos*, no. 70 (1953), 143—60. Concerns several literary problems that interested Gracián: fiction, invention, truth, wit.

HAFTER, MONROE Z. *Gracián and Perfection: Spanish Moralists of the Seventeenth Century*. Cambridge: Harvard University Press, 1966. Two-thirds of the study are concerned with Gracián and his major philosophic ideas within the framework of the seventeenth century. The study addresses itself to such issues as "the problem of moral greatness," "absolute excellence or relative superiority," "heroic artifice," and so on.

HATZFELD, HELMUT. "Three National Deformations of Aristotle: Tesauro, Gracián, Boileau." *Studi secenteschi* 2 (1961), 3—21. Excellent comparative study focusing on six problems of poetics that are shared by the three critics: poetic language, imitation, metaphor, allusion, suspense/surprise, and epithet.

HEGER, KLAUS. *Baltasar Gracián, estilo lingüístico y doctrina de valores.* . . . Zaragoza: Institución Fernando el Católico, 1960; orig. 1952, in German. A linguistic-stylistic study with an equal emphasis on the moral doctrine of Gracián.

HOMENAJE A GRACIÁN. Zaragoza: Cátedra Gracián, Institución Fernando el Católico, 1958. Diverse studies for the third centenary of Gracián's death.

HOYO, ARTURO DEL. "[Introducción]." In *Baltasar Gracián, "Obras completas.*" Estudio preliminar, edición, bibliografía y notas de Arturo del Hoyo, 2 ed. Madrid: Aguilar, 1960. An introductory survey of Gracián's life and works.

JANSEN, HELMUT. *Die Grundbegriffe des Baltasar Gracián.* (Genève: Drox, 1958, orig. 1952). A descriptive-semantic study of Gracián's ideas of the world and life; very valuable for its classification of difficult terminology.

JONES, JOSEPH R. "From Abraham to Andrenio: Observations on the Evolution of the Abraham Legend, its Diffusion in Spain, and its Relation to the Theme of the Self-Taught Philosopher." *Comparative Literature Studies* 6, no. 1 (1969), 69—101. "The plot (and other elements) of Baltasar Gracián's seventeenth-century allegorical novel *El criticón,* of which the hero is a self-taught believer, is usually thought to be based on a Morisco folktale related to the Abraham cycle. . . . But it is, in fact, a work based wholly upon Christian and classical models" (from the abstract).

KREMERS, DIETER. *Die Form der Aphorismen Graciáns.* Freiburg: University of Freiburg, 1951. Examines the external form of the aphorisms and their internal structure.

LACOSTA, FRANCISCO. "El conceptismo barroco de Baltasar Gracián en *Arte y agudeza de ingenio*" *Romance Review* 55 (1964), 85—90. Concerned with the issue of conceptismo in Gracián and in baroque aesthetics.

MATEO, J., and J. ANGUIANO. *Sobre Gracián, ensayo de criítica etnoliteraria.* Zaragoza: Colección Ruiz, 1960. Concentrates on Gracián's regional concept of literature, his strong Aragonese allegiance, and his insistent references to Aragonese writers.

MAY, T. E. "Gracián's Idea of *concepto,*" *Hispanic Review* 16 (1950), 15—41. Analysis of the conceit with the conclusion that it expresses a correspondence between objects and that its difficulty obscures reality.

———. "An Interpretation of Gracián's *Agudeza.*" *Hispanic Review* 17 (1948), 275—300. The *Agudeza* is defined as abstract and creative thought in the aesthetics of Gracián.

MAZZEO, J. A. "A Seventeenth-Century Theory of Metaphyscial Poetry," *Romanic Review* 12 (1951), 245—55. The major theoreticians—Gracián, Tesauro, Sforza-Pallavicino, Minozzi, and Pellegrini—went beyond Aristotelian doctrine on the metaphor and thereby liberated poetry from narrow rules and subject matter by emphasizing poetic creation.

METSCHIES, MICHAEL. " 'Concepto' and Zitat," *Romanische Forschungen* 79 (1967), 152—57. Discusses Gracián's statements

(*Agudeza*, Discurso 34) concerning the use as conceits of accommodated quotations from the ancients.

MONGE, FÉLIX. "Culteranismo y conceptismo a la luz de Gracián." In *Homenaje, estudios de filología e historia literaria lusohispanas e iberoamericanas.* . . .La Haya: Van Goor Zonen, 1966, pp. 355—81.

NAVARRO GONZÁLEZ, ALBERTO. "Las dos redacciones de la *Agudeza*." *Cuadernos de literatura* 4 (1948), 201—14. Both editions address themselves to the same literary issues, but the second edition contains more examples, more rules, as well as a change in prose style.

PARGA PONDAL, S. "Marcial en la preceptiva de Gracián," *Revista de archivos, bibliotecas, y museos* 20 (1930), 219—47. Gracián's main literary authority was Martial, as this study sets out to demonstrate.

PRIETO, ANTONIO. "El sujeto narrativo en 'El Criticón'." In his *Ensayo semiológico de sistemas literarios*. Barcelona: Editorial Planeta, 1972, pp. 189—253. Using the concept of semiology—the study of signs—Prieto discusses how the "subject" (i.e., in the grammatical sense of actor) of the work is given complex, structural literary forms as a narrative.

PRING-MILL, ROBERT D. F. "Some Techniques of Representation in the *Sueños* and the *Criticón*" *Bulletin of Hispanic Studies* 45 (1968), 270—84. The study is "concerned with the complex artistic reconstruction of 'reality' in two works of Golden Age fiction which . . . seem to be 'realistic' in intention, but which are patently far from 'realistic' in technique."

ROMERA NAVARRO, M. *Estudios sobre Gracián*. Austin, Texas: University of Texas Press, 1950. Treats various aspects of Gracián's writings, including humor, satiric style, allegory, and the anthology by Alfay.

————. "[Introducción]." In *Baltasar Gracián, "El Criticón"*. Edición crítica y comentada por M. Romera Navarro. Philadelphia: University of Pennsylvania Press, 1938. Provides a detailed account of the literary ideas in the *Criticón:* style, allegory as a literary device, moral and didactic intent in literature, originality, imitation and general borrowings from past literature.

SÁNCHEZ ALONSO, BENITO. "Sobre Baltasar Gracián (notas linguoestilísticas)." *Revista de filología española* 45 (1962), 161—225. A stylistic approach to Gracián's work, with a lexicographical appendix showing how Gracián deviated from the standard meaning of language.

SARMIENTO, EDWARD. "Clasificación de algunos pasajes capitales para la estética de Baltasar Gracián." *Bulletin hispanique* 37 (1935), 27—53. An index of ideas relating to Gracián's aesthetics as found in his writings.

————. "Gracián's *Agudeza y arte de ingenio.*" *Modern Language Review* 27 (1932), 280—92, 420—29. An examination of the hierarchy of conceits which placed all literary art under a single theory of conceptismo.

————. "A Preliminary Survey of Gracián's *Criticón,*" *Philological Quarterly* 18 (1933), 235—54. The survey includes a summary of the novel, as well as of Gracián's theories and of some of his literary techniques.

SCHALK, FRITZ. "Baltasar Gracián und das Ende des Siglo de Oro," *Romanische Forschungen* 54 (1940), 265—83. A discussion and evaluation of the major literary forms and terms that interested Gracián as an exemplary figure of the Spanish seventeenth century.

SCHRÖDER, GERHARDT. *Baltasar Graciáns "Criticón", eine Untersuchung zur Beziehung zwischen Manierismus and Moralistik,* München: W. Fink Verlag, 1966. A series of apparently unstructured commentaries on both the *Criticón* (sources and allegory are stressed) and the *Agudeza* (literary ideas, especially allegory). Allegory is given prominence with reference to baroque imagery and emblems, and the ideas of Alciato and Bosch are related to Gracián.

STROLLE, JON M. "Language and Morality in the *Criticón.*" *Dissertation Abstracts* 29 (1969), 4470A (Wisconsin). Words and concepts (*gusto* and *engaño-desengaño*) are described and analyzed in relationship to the moral structure of the *Criticón.*

UREMENETA, FERMÍN DE. "Sobre estética gracianesca." *Revista de ideas estéticas* 63 (1958), 217—32. Deals with Gracián's intellectuality and his doctrines of difficulty.

VOSSLER, KARL. "Introducción a Gracián." *Revista de Occidente* 13 (1935), 330—48. Studies Gracián from the point of view of style and literary ideas.

WALTON, L. B. "Two Allegorical Journeys: *Pilgrim's Progress* and *El Criticón.*" *Bulletin of Hispanic Studies* 36 (1959), 28—36. Similarities and differences between the two works are brought out with the conclusion that analogies are only coincidental.

WOODS, M. J. "Gracián, Peregrini, and the Theory of Topics." *Modern Language Review* 63, (1968), 854—63. A discussion of the classical theory of topics (*topoi,* "commonplaces") as it affects Gracián's concepts of wit in the *Agudeza;* his theory of conceits is an application of the theory of topics.

YRACHE, LUIS. "Tres alusiones curiosas en *El Criticón.*" *Papeles de Son Armadans* 43 (1966), 259—64. A study of three curious allusions and their multifaceted significance as well as their function within the context of the *Criticón.*

Index